VARSITY'S
ULTIMATE GUIDE TO
CHEERLEADING

VARSITY'S
ULTIMATE GUIDE TO
CHEERLEADING

The EDITORS of VARSITY
with REBECCA WEBBER

poppy

Little, Brown and Company
New York   Boston

By its very nature, cheerleading is a physical activity that involves risk, even when performed properly.

Do not take this risk lightly, and be constantly vigilant when practicing and performing cheerleading skills. You should take time to perfect lower-level skills and less complicated skills before attempting to move to higher and more advanced skills. Never attempt a skill outside your ability level. Always listen to your coaches, follow the rules, and ask questions if you find instructions to be unclear. Consider using the AACCA (American Association of Cheerleading Coaches and Administrators) safety rules as a guide.

Poppy

Hachette Book Group
237 Park Avenue, New York, NY 10017
Visit our website at lb-teens.com

Poppy is an imprint of Little, Brown and Company.
The Poppy name and logo are trademarks of Hachette Book Group, Inc.

The publisher is not responsible for websites (or their content) that are not owned by the publisher.

First Edition: August 2014

Library of Congress Cataloging-in-Publication Data

Webber, Rebecca.
Varsity's ultimate guide to cheerleading / Rebecca Webber and the editors of Varsity.
pages cm
ISBN 978-0-316-22728-5 (trade pbk.) — ISBN 978-0-316-22729-2 (ebook) — ISBN 978-0-316-36507-9 (library edition ebook)
1. Cheerleading. I. Title.
LB3635.W44 2014   791.6'4—dc23   2013038187

10 9 8 7 6 5 4 3 2 1
SC
Printed in China

contents

foreword

Hello and welcome to *Varsity's Ultimate Guide to Cheerleading*. At Varsity, we understand that we are the stewards of this incredibly dynamic, athletic, and high-profile activity, and we're passionate about spreading the word about cheerleading. That's why we've created this comprehensive guide for every cheerleader, parent, and coach, as well as for anyone who would like to get involved with cheerleading but isn't sure how to begin.

My passion for cheerleading is, in a word, personal. I first got involved as a "yell leader," as we were called then, at the University of Oklahoma. I later launched the company that has become Varsity, the leader in all things cheerleading and a one-stop shop for everything cheerleaders need to maximize their experience. Varsity offers the very best camps, competitions, uniforms, and spirit gear, as well as an unparalleled amount of information about cheerleading skills and lifestyle, fundraising options, and community service.

Varsity's Ultimate Guide to Cheerleading covers all these topics and can guide you from your very first tryout to your senior year in college. We've included practical, hands-on advice from former cheerleaders from some of the best teams in the country who have dedicated much of their lives to cheerleading. There are also plenty of tips from active cheerleaders of all ages who are currently firing up fans at football and basketball games and in competition arenas all across the United States. For example, you'll find information on preparing for tryouts, planning your year, and excelling at competition, as well as key tips on skills and stunts.

We tell you about the incredible impact cheerleaders have had on the world; you'll be inspired by what some of these individuals and teams have accomplished. Because, as all cheerleaders know, there's more to this great activity than cheers. This guide explains the characteristics of great cheerleaders—attributes such as leadership, spirit, commitment, kindness, and motivation. Cheerleaders serve their communities, compete with the best, and are the ultimate ambassadors for their schools.

Once you've absorbed all the great information, photographs, and inspiring examples in these pages, visit us online at varsity.com for even more, including videos of outstanding cheerleaders and teams in action.

Enjoy!

JEFF WEBB

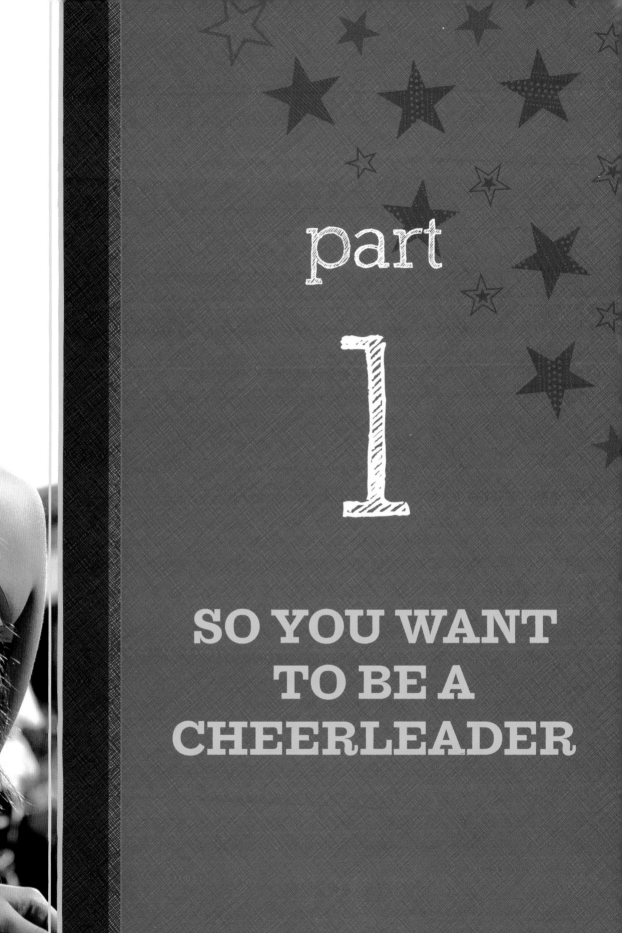

part

1

SO YOU WANT TO BE A CHEERLEADER

what makes a great cheerleader?

Maybe you first noticed cheerleaders on the sidelines of a football game, shouting support for their team and having a blast. Or you might have clicked on the YouTube video of the cheerleader breaking the world record for the most back handsprings. Or maybe you were channel-surfing on a Saturday afternoon and came across an intense competition with squads performing cheers, dances, jumps, and incredible stunts. You were probably wowed, and wondered: How did that girl do a perfect toe touch? How does that human pyramid stay up? And where do cheerleaders get all that energy?

Cheerleading is where athleticism meets showmanship. It requires strength, balance, rhythm, tumbling skills, and enthusiasm to spare. At top levels, squads are on par with acrobatic troupes. But no cheerleader started out knowing how to do a full up to a liberty. Newcomers start with the basics: easy chants and arm motions, simple jumps, and beginner stunts.

Whether you're a newbie or already part of a championship squad, *Varsity's Ultimate Guide to Cheerleading* can help you become the absolute best cheerleader you can be. This book provides tips on everything from nailing your very first tryout to winning a cheerleading championship.

But before we get started with all that, there's a question we have to ask: *Do you have what it takes to be a great cheerleader?* How many of the following qualities do you have?

The Ingredients

CONFIDENCE

Having faith in yourself and your abilities is the most important key to success in anything you try in life—from taking the SAT to performing your best stunt. "You can always tell who is self-confident; they're ready to go get 'em," says Allie Farrell, a cheerleader for Western Kentucky University's coed squad. Good preparation, and lots and lots of practice, is the way to build up your confidence.

When you learn a new cheer, a jump, or a tumbling skill, practice it as much as possible. Go over the words and the motions, again and again. If it's a tough jump or dance sequence you are trying to master, do ten of them every day to strengthen your muscles...and your self-assurance. When it's time to show your stuff in front of a crowd, you'll be ready.

After all, cheerleaders are high-profile, and when you're cheering at a game or in a competition, people *will* be watching. You can't second-guess yourself: *Were my wrists straight in that high V? Is my heel stretch high enough?* You have to be secure in your abilities. When you know exactly what you're capable of, you can bring it—every time!

SPIRIT

Also known as enthusiasm. Also known as energy. Cheerleaders are responsible for pumping up the crowd—even when it's pouring rain and your team is down by twenty-one points. You might be cold and disappointed, but don't even think about packing up your poms. This is the time to ramp it up with your favorite chants and to dance in the rain to the tunes of the marching band. You'll keep cheering until the final whistle is blown. "It's easy when you love the program or school you're cheering for," says Ryan Martin, a longtime cheerleader, most recently for the University of Alabama.

Team pride is essential. It has to *matter* to you whether the team wins or loses. Your enthusiasm will ignite the people in the stands, who will fire up the athletes on the field or the court.

PERSONALITY

Cheerleaders should be friendly and outgoing with everyone they meet, especially when in uniform! Remember, you represent your school and squad. "We go to a lot of events, and we have to interact and talk to people," says Jacob Benedict, who cheered all four years at the University of Central Florida. You should be comfortable engaging in conversation with anyone from the school principal to the captain of a rival squad. And you also need to work well with all the other members of your squad. "Cheerleading is about teamwork," Jacob says.

Naturally, you can't become BFFs with everyone in the world, but you should treat all people with kindness and respect. Make it your mission to encourage the entire student body to take part in spirit- or service-related activities. Reach out to other teams and clubs—from the honor society to the drama club to the yearbook staff—to work together on projects that benefit the school or other important causes. Cheerleaders from Mascoutah High School in Illinois partner with the girls' volleyball team each October for a huge event to promote breast cancer awareness. "Cheerleaders should get along well with everyone, especially other female athletes," says the Mascoutah coach, Laurie Wager. "We love the volleyball team. We go to their games and cheer for them."

PHYSICAL FITNESS

Cheerleading is physically demanding, and you shouldn't even consider it unless you're ready to sweat! "A good cheerleader has to be a good athlete," says Blake Johnson, who cheered for the University of Kentucky and also played football, basketball, and baseball, and ran track in high school.

Whether you're getting ready for your first tryout or you're already familiar with the view from the top of the pyramid, some simple rules apply.

★ **Exercise:** Walk, run, dance, swim, bike, or hit the gym or the weight room regularly. But do so safely. There's a right way and a wrong way to get in shape. Never strain or push yourself beyond a reasonable limit. If you're just starting out, or if you're ready to take your skills to the next level, sign up for professional training with a cheer or gymnastics coach, ideally one who is certified by the American Association of Cheerleading Coaches and Administrators (AACCA).

★ **Eat Well:** A healthy diet is imperative. Eat regular meals that include lots of fruits and vegetables, whole grains, and healthy proteins. And if you have questions about proper nutrition, sit down with your family doctor or the school nurse to sketch out a food plan that will keep you in top form for practices, games, and competitions.

★ **Sleep:** As a cheerleader, you'll demand a lot from your body, and in return, it needs adequate rest. Sleep gives your body a chance to recharge itself. It's also good for your mind and helps you remember everything you're learning in school.

RESPONSIBILITY

Cheerleading is a commitment, and you need to be ready, willing, and able to show up when you're supposed to—at practices, games, pep rallies, fundraising events, special appearances, and competitions. "You have to take responsibility and do everything that's required of you," says Caity Hinshaw, a cheerleader at Indiana University. Routines and cheers are built upon the entire group working together.

PASSION

When you really care about what you're doing, it's obvious to the people around you, and that kind of enthusiasm is contagious. It helps all of you work harder toward your goals—so that someday soon everyone on the squad will have a back handspring, and all your team members can hit solid liberties.

The best cheerleaders are happy to be involved in the squad's activities—whether decorating the school for homecoming week, volunteering at a walkathon, perfecting a routine for the pep rally, or leading the crowd at a basketball game. "Passion helps you stay positive all the time and shine a good light on your program," says Ryan Martin.

That *doesn't* mean you have to give up your whole life for cheerleading, of course. Plenty of cheerleaders are also deeply involved with other things—like the school musical, the science fair, the softball team, or the student council.

But you just won't be a good cheerleader if you aren't passionate about it. So if you get a major charge from the thought of putting on that uniform and doing your thing with your teammates...grab those poms and cheer on!

LEADERSHIP

At a game or competition, cheerleaders command attention. All eyes will be on you when you draw the crowd into a chant at a basketball game or take the floor at halftime or at a competition. "If you're smiling all the time and look like you're having fun, people will feed off that," says Ronnie Patrick, who cheered at Morehead State University and the University of Tennessee.

But people will also be following your lead at other times: like when you're standing in line at the concession stand or studying in the library for your chemistry exam. As long as you're a cheerleader—whether you're wearing your uniform or not—you're someone who should set a great example by acting the way you'd like everyone else to act. This means doing the right thing (even when it's hard!) and making decisions that will make the world a better place.

Always remember: someday a little kid will be watching *you* at a football game, on YouTube, or on ESPN and will think, *I want to be like her (or him)!* And the cycle of great cheerleading will continue.

the *history*
of cheerleading

Cheerleading has been around for more than 115 years, and while the spirit behind the moves remains the same, a lot has changed, too. Check out our time line and learn how cheerleading has gone from an all-male, collegiate-only pursuit to a female-dominated, globally recognized athletic activity.

The HISTORY of CHEERLEADING

1898:

In 1898, the University of Minnesota was on a losing streak. The school newspaper put out a plea for help in getting the crowd enthused. In response, a medical student named Johnny Campbell assembled a group to energize the team and the crowd. He rallied the team to victory with the first organized cheer: "RAH, RAH, RAH! SKI-U-MAH! HOO-RAH! HOO-RAH! VARSITY! VARSITY! MINN-E-SO-TAH!" Minnesota won the game, and Campbell and his "yell leaders" were credited with cheering the team to victory. Cheerleading was born.

1910:

The University of Illinois introduced "homecoming" festivities.

1920s:

College women began to participate in cheerleading, and cheerleaders at the University of Minnesota added tumbling to their routines.

1927:

The first book about cheerleading, *Just Yells* by Willis Bugbee, was published by the Bugbee Company of Syracuse, New York.

1940s:

With many young men off serving in World War II, girls became more active in cheerleading and were soon the majority participants in the activity.

1946:

Lawrence R. Herkimer, a cheerleader at Southern Methodist University, developed his signature "Herkie" jump. The nickname stuck for the move and for the man.

1948:

Herkimer, then a teacher at Southern Methodist University, held the first summer cheerleading clinic at Sam Houston State Teachers College (now called State University) in Huntsville, Texas; fifty-three students attended.

1950:

Two years after creating the first NFL performance group, Robert Olmstead founded California Specialty Camps and held its first summer camps in the mountains near Santa Cruz, California, to train girls to perform as majorettes at San Francisco 49ers games.

1951:

Herkimer formally incorporated the National Cheerleaders Association (NCA) and began to offer one-day clinics for cheerleaders in the fall. Cheerleader Supply Company was founded in Dallas, Texas, to provide skirts and sweaters, chenille letters, spirit ribbons, bull horns, and the like for cheerleaders across the country.

1952:

NCA's *Megaphone* magazine was first published and mailed four times per year; it remained in circulation until 1982.

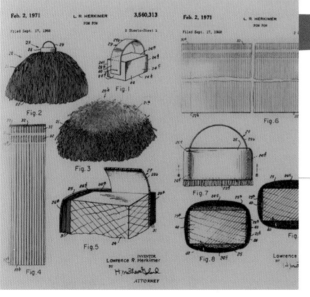

1956:

Herkimer invented the pom pon— also known as the shake-a-roo— out of crepe paper and a stick. An improved version—updated with a hidden handle and vinyl streamers—was patented in 1971.

1958:

Herkimer's first two books, *Champion Cheers* and *Pep Rallies, Skits and Stunts*, were published.

1959:

The growth of dance and drill teams inspired a merging of dance, drill, and cheer to create pom pon girls (today's "songleaders"). California Specialty Camps inaugurated a camp program to meet the needs of this unique activity, which was popular in western states.

1960s:

Herkie and his staff prepped for the camp season.

1965:

NCA's first Cheerleader Supply Company Catalog was printed and mailed.

1966:

NCA created the spirit stick to recognize team effort, ethusiasm, and genuine cheerleader spirit.

1967:

Peewee and youth league cheerleading developed.

1970s:

Partner stunts, pyramids, dance incorporations, and elite tumbling became popular.

1972:

★ This year marked the passage of Title IX, providing equal athletic opportunities for women. Title IX encouraged schools to have more women's teams, which increased the overall athleticism of female students.

★ After graduating from Princeton University, Michael Olmstead joined his father, Robert, in the family business, California Specialty Camps, further developing the camp curriculum by adding leadership and rally workshops. The next year, he taught the first mascot camp with the help of a mime and experts from the character program at Disneyland, specialists in nonverbal communication.

1974:

Universal Cheerleaders Association (UCA) was founded by Jeff Webb, former cheerleader at the University of Oklahoma, then vice president and general manager at NCA. He was joined by his brother Greg in 1976. UCA's curriculum was based on partner stunt and pyramid technique, private coaching, team building, and game day. Webb introduced new stunt, pyramid, and crowd techniques.

1975:

★ The cheer routine was born when UCA instructors Jerry Starnes and Kris Shepherd combined music with cheer skills at the opening of a university training camp. The first routine was performed to the theme song from the movie *Rocky*.
★ The NCA All-American award for individuals debuted.

1976:

★ UCA demonstrated the liberty and tossing stunts at its summer camps.
★ California Specialty Camps changed its name to United Spirit Association (USA) to emphasize the scope of its camp programs, including drill, pom, and cheer.

1979:

The first high school cheerleading championship was held in Memphis, Tennessee. State winners from eight states were invited to compete in the championship tournament.

1980s:

New safety guidelines were adopted, creating height restrictions for pyramids and prohibiting the use of mini trampolines. These requirements provided universal standards for cheerleading and made safety the number one concern for cheerleaders. Award-winning camp squads began performing at bowl games and parades. Cheer competitions became popular.

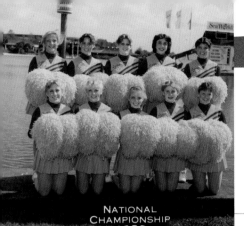

NATIONAL
CHAMPIONSHIP
1980

1980:

★ UCA inaugurated the National High School Cheerleading Championship, held at SeaWorld.

★ Jeff Webb and Kris Shepherd founded Universal Dance Association (UDA) as Universal Dance/Pom Association (UDPA) to provide educational training for what were then called drill teams. UDA coined the term *dance teams* to better describe the activity.

1983:

ESPN began broadcasting the National High School Cheerleading Championship, which previously aired on a network called TVS; today, both ESPN and ESPN2 air UCA's annual high school, collegiate, all star, and dance championships.

1984:

★ USA produced its first Super Bowl Pregame theme show with dancers, mascots, and six hundred cheerleaders!

★ The first organized gym for cheerleading, NCA's Cheerobics Center, opened in Dallas, Texas.

1986:

★ The first USA Nationals was conducted. This event brings together cheer, song, mascot, short flag, color guard, drum major, and dance/drill teams. The USA signature "Crowdleader Team" division was created.

★ NCA Superstar dance/drill team officers from across the country opened the 60th Anniversary Macy's Thanksgiving Day Parade in New York City. In 1989, NCA cheerleaders joined the parade program, and in 1994, UCA and UDA also became part of the yearly event.

★ UCA and UDA staff performed at the two-hundred-year anniversary of the Statue of Liberty.

1987:

★ The UCA and UDA performed for the first time at the Lord Mayor of Westminster's Big Parade, now called the London New Year's Day Parade. Today, UCA, UDA, NCA, NDA, and USA (United Spirit Association) are a part of the annual event, with more than a thousand participants.

★ UCA created the first cheer safety manual and organization, American Association of Cheer Coaches and Advisors (now Administrators). The following year, AACCA, in conjunction with UCA, developed the first safety program for coaches.

★ NCA became the first organization to administer a competition for all star teams.

1988:

Spirit goes global! Jeff Webb's organization introduced cheer training programs in Japan and the United Kingdom, and later in other European countries, Latin America, Oceania, and Africa.

1990s:

Participation in camps and competitions skyrocketed; ESPN broadcast UCA shows around the world.

1990:

UCA and UDA performed on the Muscular Dystrophy Association telethon; since then the groups have contributed more than one million dollars to the association.

1995:

★ *American Cheerleader* magazine debuted.
★ Disney World became the cheer mecca of the United States when UCA moved its events to the Walt Disney World® Resort in Florida.

1996:

NCA cheerleaders participated in the opening ceremonies of the Summer Olympics in Atlanta, Georgia, and the NCA Collegiate National Championship, held in Daytona Beach, Florida, was televised on NBC. The championship is now televised on CBS Sports Network.

2000s:

★ Cheerleaders continued to refine their skills and test their limits.

★ Hollywood released *Bring It On*, featuring rival cheering squads in California and starring Kirsten Dunst and Eliza Dushku. A UCA high school event provided inspiration for the film's writers, and the movie went on to become a cult classic and inspired multiple sequels.

2004:

The USASF/IASF hosted the first World Cheerleading Championships for all star/club teams.

2005:

★ International education programs and world championship participation accelerated, with about eleven new national federations forming each year.

★ Varsity Wired, now called Varsity TV, was created. It is an online home to 45,000 videos and continues to grow.

2006:

The first cheer-based reality TV show, *Cheerleader Nation,* aired. The program followed the Dunbar High School cheerleading squad on their journey to the national championship.

2008:

High school cheerleader Sarah Cronk created the Sparkle Effect.*

2008:

USA Cheer, the national governing body for sport cheerleading, was created to help grow and develop interest and participation in cheer throughout the United States, promote safety and safety education for cheer in the United States, and represent the United States of America in international cheer competitions.

2009

★ National School Spirit Day was created to recognize the positive impact that cheerleaders and dancers can have in their schools and communities.

★ NCA created a partnership with Make-A-Wish to raise money for critically ill children nationwide.

* See Chapter Eleven for more information on the Sparkle Effect.

2011:

★ Varsity partnered with St. Jude Children's Research Hospital to support its lifesaving mission of finding cures for children fighting cancer and other deadly diseases. Each summer, 350,000 cheerleading and dance team camp attendees are asked to send five donation letters to friends and family members. In the first two years of partnership, Varsity raised more than one million dollars for St. Jude.

★ The National High School Sports-Related Injury Surveillance Study listed cheerleading as one of the safest sports, second only to swimming.

★ College STUNT's first season included twenty teams. This new format for cheer focuses on the technical and the athletic components of cheer in head-to-head competition. STUNT meets requirements for NCAA emerging-sport status.

★ *Bring It On: The Musical*, based on the film, premiered. Varsity assisted with choreography on the show, and the cast wore Varsity Spirit Fashion uniforms. Some of the show's cast were Varsity camp instructors!

2013:

★ ICU was recognized as the worldwide governing body by SportAccord, securing ICU's place in the international sports community.

★ myVarsity mobile app launched. The first of its kind, myVarsity enables high school cheerleaders and dancers to achieve goals and earn pins at Varsity summer camps.

★ *Game On*, the first book in Varsity's original fiction series, launched.

★ Varsity joined forces with Partnership for a Healthier America to help fight childhood obesity. Through Cheer for a Healthier America, Varsity encourages high school cheer and dance teams to host "Play Days" at local elementary schools to encourage physical activity.

2012:

Bring It On: The Musical hit Broadway! The show was nominated for a Tony in the Best Musical category.

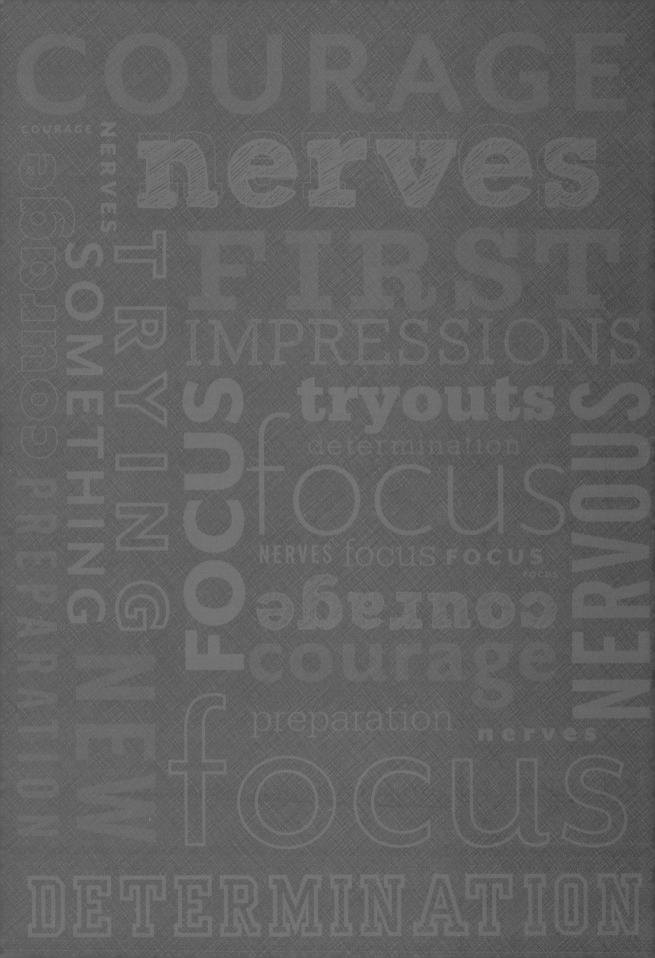

making
the team

I f you've made it this far into the book, you might *already* be a cheerleader, or maybe you're hoping to become one. For those who are just starting out, the available cheerleading options will depend on your age, location, and ability level, so it's smart to scout out the possibilities. There are lots of them—from competition-only squads to community-based programs to cheering for your own school.

Total newbies might consider taking a class to learn the basics. There are gyms that offer classes for all ages and all skill levels.

Once you're ready to join a squad, see if you can sit in on a practice or watch them at a game so you'll know what you're getting yourself into. Request information from the coach about the schedule for practices, games, and competitions; the overall time commitment; and how far you'll be able to advance if you stick with cheerleading over the long term.

Various cheerleading opportunities are available in most places throughout the country.

Types of Cheerleading Squads

TOWN RECREATIONAL LEAGUES

Check with your town's Parks and Recreation department to find out if it offers cheerleading. Lots of rec departments do, and some welcome kids as young as three years old! Participation in a rec league is a great way to learn basic cheerleading elements, and to make friends from outside your school and neighborhood, because kids from all around town can join these squads. You'll probably cheer for the rec center's football and basketball teams, so the experience will involve practices, games, and possibly competitions.

ALL STAR

If you already know you want to be serious about cheerleading, check out an all star program. It's similar to taking lessons at a competitive dance studio or learning to ride and show horses by training at an equestrian stable; you generally pay tuition. A tryout starts with an evaluation of your cheerleading skills, and you're then placed on a squad based on your age and current ability.

You attend practices a few times a week to learn all aspects of cheerleading—including dance, jumps, tumbling, and stunting.

All star squads do *not* cheer for other sports teams. The main focus (besides having a ton of fun with your cheer friends) is competition. All star squads go up against squads from similar gyms across the country. So if you plan to go this route, be ready to put in some serious practice time, and then bring it to the blue mats!

SCHOOL
★ Elementary

Some elementary schools offer cheerleading, but since many are not part of competitive sports leagues, lots of younger girls now turn to all star programs to "get their cheer on." If you are one of the lucky ones whose elementary school has a beginner squad, this is the perfect

place to start learning age- and ability-appropriate skills, things like cartwheels, shoulder straddles, and a solid high V. You'll probably cheer for your school's basketball team or another sport, so you'll also be strengthening friendships with your classmates and showing your school spirit while improving your cheerleading technique.

★ Middle School/Junior High

Most middle or junior high schools have cheerleading squads, and you can spend these years learning harder skills, like back handsprings and extension preps, and more complicated cheers and routines. You'll be a part of the school sports scene. If your junior high has a football team, your cheer responsibilities will begin at the start of the school year, when football season opens. You may also cheer for the basketball program. Cheer tryouts and first practices will most likely take place at the end of the previous school year or over the summer, giving you a head start on getting to know the other members of your squad.

★ High School

As a high school cheerleader, you'll be shouting on the sidelines at all the big games, performing at halftime and at pep rallies, and participating in lots of other school events. Your squad may have community- or school-service requirements, like greeting visitors on parents' nights. You're a goodwill ambassador and spokesperson for the school, so it's especially important to be a good role model.

High school is definitely a balancing act. You will have other extracurricular activities, as well as a grade point average to maintain. But cheerleading may be one of your biggest time commitments. Besides cheer practices and games, your squad may compete on a local, regional, or national level, and this can require many additional hours of practice.

Even if you don't compete, high school may be when you reach your full cheering potential. You're stronger than ever, possibly with lots of experience. Your squad may go for elite stunts—that standing back tuck!—more complicated routines, and more sophisticated stunts, like basket tosses, liberties, and scorpions.

★ College

Girls and guys who cheer at this level mean business! Many have trained their whole lives to get here. Vying for a place on these squads is, of course, intense. It might be a little easier to land a spot on a squad that doesn't compete nationally or cheer for a nationally ranked sports team.

At college games, the crowds are bigger, away games might involve a plane ride, and depending on what division your school plays in, you might even find yourself smiling into a television camera. Lots of college squads are coed, and due to the added strength of the guys, you could be attempting the hardest stunts of your life.

Some college squads are seriously competitive, which means that instead of heading home over winter break, you stay on campus for practices to prepare for Nationals. And the college cheerleader's schedule isn't that much lighter the rest of the year. "Be prepared to set aside at least an hour or two every day for something related to cheerleading," advises Ryan Martin, a former college cheerleader. That's because besides games, practices, and workouts (to stay strong, flexible, and in shape by working with a trainer, running sprints, or doing circuits), college cheerleaders also act as ambassadors of the school—for example, chatting up alumni at a party held by the university president. "It's not about just cheering games anymore," explains former cheerleader Blake Johnson. "You're an image for your school."

STUNT

If you're in it because you love to perform the most difficult jumps and tosses and the hardest tumbling—*and* you've got a serious competitive streak—STUNT may be the sport for you!

School cheerleading is a broad athletic activity, and it usually doesn't meet the narrow requirements that officially define a sport, which are set out by the Office for Civil Rights, part of the U.S. Department of Education. One of the basic definitions of a sport is that its sole purpose is competition. The sticking point is that cheerleaders have a much broader role within athletics, and competition is just one part of the activity, which also includes building school spirit, supporting athletics, and providing leadership. But cheer experts have done something about this issue by developing STUNT.

STUNT leaves out the crowd-leading and game-day elements of cheerleading and pits squads directly against one another on skills. But it takes the competitive aspect even further. STUNT teams all learn the same compulsory routines, then perform them at the same time, right next to one another on the mat. This way, judges—and even people in the crowd—can easily figure out who deserves to win.

Each STUNT game is divided into four quarters, and squads are required to perform a total of ten to sixteen thirty-second routines. These cover partner stunts, tosses, and pyramids; group jumps and tumbling; and combinations of all these. Objective scoring determines the winning squad. Also, each athlete wears a number on her uniform to track individual performances, which helps determine who makes All-American.

"STUNT will create even more opportunities for a large number of female athletes to get involved in a spring sport at the high school and college levels," says Bill Seely, executive director of USA Cheer and one of the founders of STUNT. It is available at the college level, where teams can play twelve to sixteen games per season, and at high schools, where they can have eight to ten games.

The sport's popularity is increasing. It launched on the college level in 2011, with twenty-two teams participating. By 2013, STUNT was the fastest-growing female sport in the country. And it's being embraced on the high school level as well, with dozens of teams starting up nationwide.

The NCAA is evaluating STUNT for "emerging sport" status, and its founders expect it to be sanctioned as an official sport—thus eligible for scholarship funds that could be used toward the schools' Title IX requirements.

Getting Started

Let's be honest: cheerleading tryouts aren't the most fun part of the season. They can be big-time nerve-racking, because the outcome will determine your cheer experience over the next year or so. The good news: there are many ways to make the process smoother. You'll want to start prepping before the first day of the tryout clinic, because the more you know, the more confident you'll be, and that's guaranteed to give you an edge. Here are some tips for getting ready, both physically and mentally, for the big audition.

CHECK 'EM OUT

If possible, spend some time watching the squad you hope to join. Attend games, competitions, and even practices if the coaches say it's okay. No two cheerleading squads are exactly alike. Each has a vibe, a style, a personality all its own. This will be most evident when the team members are cheering together at a game or in a competition—operating in their element—as opposed to when they are focused on running a clinic or a practice. Your goal in observing the squad is to check out the following cheerleading skills:

★ **Cheers & Chants:** Note the pitch and volume of their voices and the pace of their words.

★ **Motions:** High Vs and low Vs are a given. But keep an eye out for any other motions unique to a squad—such as a two-fingered V for the Vikings, or pinky-and-pointer-finger horns for the Longhorns.

★ **Jumps:** Does everyone have a stellar toe touch? Or have they made the Herkie their signature jump?

★ **Dancing:** Do they execute precision routines to the tunes of the marching band? Do they incorporate hip-hop tricks? Or perform to fast-paced electronic music? Maybe all three!

★ **Tumbling:** Does everyone on the squad have a back handspring? Or are there tumbling "specialists," while the rest of the squad stunts or dances?

★ **Stunting:** Does the squad put up stunts, and if so, at what level? Do the top girls full down or straight cradle out of an extension? Do they spend a lot of time on stunts compared with the other aspects of cheerleading?

Whip out your phone and record a few videos of your future squad's performance. Back at home, see if you can pick up a few of the cheers or chants to practice on your own. Think about your own strengths as a cheerleader, and figure out what you still need to work on for your best chance at making the team.

Get the Details

WHERE AND WHEN?

Find out the dates, times, and locations for all pre-tryout clinics...and write them down. Clear your schedule so you can be there for every minute of the clinics; missing even an hour of the instruction could put you at a disadvantage when it's time to show 'em what you can do.

Be punctual. Coaches and captains will notice those who arrive after the start time. After all, it's reasonable for them to conclude that a person who is tardy for tryout clinics is more likely to show up late for games and practices.

Organize any paperwork, like a signed parental release form or a doctor's form that shows you've had a physical, before the tryout clinic begins.

WHAT EXACTLY HAPPENS AT THE TRYOUT?

There's no standard format for a cheerleading tryout. You may be brought before the judges alone, or with one or more other contenders. Usually, outside spectators are not allowed (sorry, Mom!).

You will probably be expected to perform at least one cheer and some jumps (all of which will have been taught and practiced at the tryout clinics). You may also have to perform a dance routine, some basic tumbling, and some partner stunts. Once you've executed all the required elements, you might be allowed to show off any additional tumbling or stunting skills you have.

In some cases, depending on how many people are going out for the squad, there will be a first cut, which means some girls and guys will be eliminated on the first go-round, and the rest will come back a second time to perform the skills again and perhaps try some new ones.

Typically, the judging panel will consist of people with cheering expertise. Sometimes, outside judges are brought in, perhaps from a neighboring school or dance academy or cheerleading gym.

REAL CHEERLEADERS
REAL ANSWERS

What do you do to keep from getting nervous before a tryout, a big game, or a major competition?

"First, I keep **running the routine** through my head again and again to help me focus. If I'm worried about a stunt or a tumbling pass or something like that, **I think about a time when I hit it perfectly**, so I feel confident about it."
—ALEX

"I listen to all star cheerleading music and **stay to myself during warm-ups**."
—ALYSSA

"Before tryouts we all get together and critique each other's jumps, motions, etc. Before a competition, we **do a silly huddle cheer** to get all our nerves out."
—JESSE

"Practice, practice, **practice**…and **breathe**."
—BETHANY

"I go over the routine and I have one of **my friends judge** me!"
—CLARA

"I make sure my team is **well prepared.** If everyone is **confident,** it decreases my nerves!"
—JOANNE

"I tell myself to let it all out on the mat and to **have no regrets!**"
—ALEXA

"Listen to our 'pumped up' playlist and sing along to it with my squad."
—BROOKE

"I always think about all the **good times** my team and I have had."
—CAITLYN

"Just **stay calm** and let my body do the work, not my mind."
—DRUANNE

KNOW THE ODDS

It's not a bad idea to know up front what your chances are—realistically—of making the team. This will be based not only on your ability in comparison to the other candidates but also on the squad's size limit and their current needs. Here are some things to consider:

★ How many squads are there, and who is eligible to cheer at which level? Is eligibility based on age or grade, or are the teams assembled based on ability?

★ Do the people on last year's squad automatically get a spot, or does everyone have to try out again? Even if it's the latter, those with more years of cheerleading experience will probably have a bit of an advantage over newbies. But if you're the one trying to break in for the first time, just do the best you can and keep the faith. The results of almost every tryout include a few surprises.

★ How many spots are the judges looking to fill? If two hundred girls are vying for three spots, approach the tryout with cautious optimism. Take your shot, but remember there are just so many openings and no guarantees.

★ Does the squad choose any alternates (who can step in if ever a regular squad member can't attend a game or competition, or if someone gets injured)?

Warming Up

Whenever you're about to get your cheer on, you need to warm up first. Stretching will get your muscles ready for the tumbling and jumps you'll need to do. Your tryout instructors will show you appropriate stretches and other warm-up exercises before you begin jumping, tumbling, and running through the routines. On the following pages are some basic stretches that can be the foundation of your warm-up routine. Remember to never stretch cold. Try jogging laps around the gym or jumping rope to get your muscles warm.

STRETCHING

Any stretching, particularly partner stretching, should be performed in a controlled manner, under the supervision of a coach or trainer.

SEATED HAMSTRING STRETCH

1.

While sitting on the ground, straighten out your legs and reach forward to grab your feet. Reach as far as you can, without being uncomfortable, in order to feel a stretch.

2.

Now reach for your toes and pull them back toward you off the ground.

STANDING HAMSTRING STRETCH

1.

Spread your feet apart a little wider than your shoulders and slowly reach down toward the ground.

2.

Keep your legs straight and reach over your right toe.
Do the same stretch, but switch to your left toe.

HIP AND LOWER-BACK STRETCH

1.

Stand with your feet much wider apart than your shoulders. Slowly place your hands down to your knees and pull your left shoulder back while pushing your right leg back. Do the same on the other side.

2.

Step your right foot out in front of your left. Keep your right knee in line with your ankle and reach down and touch the ground. You should feel a stretch in your hip. Do the same on the other side.

QUAD STRETCH

1. *Stand on your left leg. Grab your right foot and gently pull back toward you until you feel a stretch in the front of your thigh. Make sure you keep your knee in line with your hip.*

2. *Repeat stretch standing on your right leg and pulling back your left foot.*

ARMS AND SHOULDERS

Gently pull your right arm across your chest with your left arm until you feel a good stretch in your shoulder. Switch sides.

Bend your right arm back behind your head and gently pull back toward the left side of your body. Switch sides.

PARTNER STRETCHING

PARTNER 1: *Stand with your arms behind your back. Relax and let your partner pull your arms closer together.*

PARTNER 2: *Gently pull your partner's arms closer together while keeping them in line with her shoulders. Make sure you go slowly! Make sure you stop when she tells you to!*

PARTNER 1: *Kneel down on your right knee and offer your left leg up to your partner. Grab behind her legs for support.*

PARTNER 2: *Grab the left ankle of your partner. Keep her leg straight while pulling it slowly toward you. Make sure you stop when she tells you to! Do the same on the other side.*

YOU'VE GOT THIS *in the* BAG

Here's what you'll want to have handy at tryouts:

★ WATER BOTTLE

★ A HEALTHY SNACK: FRUIT, NUTS, OR A GRANOLA OR PROTEIN BAR

★ HAIRBRUSH

★ EXTRA HAIR CLIPS, ELASTICS, AND HAIR SPRAY

★ MAKEUP FOR TOUCH-UPS

★ PACK OF TISSUES

★ NAIL FILE OR CLIPPERS

★ CLEAR DEODORANT

★ YOUR FAVORITE GOOD LUCK CHARM. Don't worry, no one will laugh. Chances are you won't be the only one with a lucky stuffed koala or two-dollar bill tucked into your bag.

★ If you want to leave nothing to chance, you can also pack a COMPLETE SPARE OUTFIT, so your performance won't be derailed by a ripped seam or a spilled drink.

JUMPING

Here's a guarantee: cheerleading jumps* are not as easy as they look. When top cheerleaders execute those perfect toe touches, it may seem as though they've got wings on their cheer shoes, but the truth is, getting that much air is a function of a whole lot of strength developed through practice. Focus on your approach technique and landing at tryouts. If you're a newbie, don't worry if your jumps aren't perfect. You will learn proper jumping techniques at camp.

TUMBLING

If you've been taking gymnastics since the minute you learned to walk, you've probably already mastered the tumbling requirements of the squad you hope to join. But for most people, these skills can take time—and usually the assistance of a good coach—to learn. Perform only the tumbling skills you are already very comfortable with—it's better to show a simple skill with good execution than a skill you are not certain you can land.

STUNTING

Stunts and pyramids* are fairly unique to cheerleading, so when you're just starting out, you'll need to learn everything—from when to bend and straighten your legs to how to properly support a girl by her shoe. Don't worry! You won't be expected to master a basket toss on your first day. Just keep it simple. Some tryouts do not require stunting at all, and you will learn the proper fundamentals of stunting at camp.

* See Chapter Five for photos and detailed descriptions of jumps and stunts.

DANCING

After you learn the dance routine in the tryout clinic, see if you can download a copy of the music so that you can practice it at home. Invite over some friends who are also going out for the squad. You can help one another perfect the routine on your own time, which will make you feel much more confident when it's time to go before the judges.

CHEERING

Probably the most important element of the tryouts! Write down the words and the accompanying motions so that you can get them down pat. Practice them over and over at home, in front of a mirror and for your family or friends. (You might as well get used to performing for a crowd!) Have someone record your efforts with a phone or video camera so that you can see what you look like and correct any problems, like a too-wide high V or a too-soft voice. Run through your routines in your tryout attire. Were there any awkward surprises, like bra straps showing or shorts riding up? Better to fix these issues before your tryout.

TRIUMPH *at* TRYOUTS

Whether you're trying out for the very first time or you've done it every year since you were six, remember that judges are focusing on your *potential* to be a really great cheerleader. That means you don't have to be perfect in every way, but you should already have some building blocks in place. "We look for someone with a loud voice, strong motions, good jumps, and the potential to tumble," says Josh McCurdy, a former college cheerleader, longtime coach, and instructor for UCA. "We're also looking for coordination and athletic ability." Josh has helped select cheerleaders for squads at Greenup County High School and various colleges. Here are his other tryout tips.

LOOK THE PART

"You should show up looking like you're going to cheer a game—wearing school colors, with a bow in your hair. As a judge, I want to see what you'll look like on the sideline," says Josh. So skip the basketball shorts or the crazy paisley socks (even if they are your lucky ones).

PLAY UP YOUR STRENGTHS

A strong tumbler or a top-notch jumper will always stand out, but squads need people who can fill all sorts of roles. Some people can base or back-spot even if they can't do a cartwheel. "A volleyball player who has never cheered before could make the cut," says Josh, "because she's tall, strong, and athletic."

BE WELL ROUNDED

If you're not a specialist in any one thing, just do the best you can in *every* area. Most judging follows a score sheet, with different categories for skills like motions, spirit, and stunts. "You have to score average to good in everything, and maybe even above average," says Josh.

KEEP AN ATTITUDE IN CHECK

Make sure you follow the rules, don't complain, don't push the limits, and show that you can be a team player. "You don't want someone who's going to be an issue because they are negative or they don't like to work hard," says Josh. "A bad attitude can ruin the atmosphere of the program."

SMILE THROUGH ANY MISTAKES

You're halfway through the cheer when, OMG, you forget the words! "You're okay," says Josh. "Smile through it—even if you miss every single motion. Just clap, smile through it, and look happy."

Get Ready

Find out in advance what you will need to wear to tryouts. It might be your gym uniform, or shorts and a T-shirt in specific colors. If no dress code is specified, err on the side of simplicity. This is not the time to express your super-unique fashion sense and rock something trendy or unusual. You want the judges to envision you fitting right in with all the other members of the squad.

Unless you are otherwise instructed, your tryout attire should consist of the following:

★ Well-fitting (not too tight, not baggy) athletic shorts in a solid hue—ideally one of your school colors, to highlight your school spirit!

★ A T-shirt or tank top that is comfortable but not oversized. Solid colors or school spirit wear only. No funny sayings, crazy patterns, or pictures of glittery dragonflies. Keep it neat and simple.

★ Clean sneakers with good traction, flexibility, and support.

★ Athletic socks that match the preferences of the squad. Some like taller socks; others don't want to see them at all.

Other tips on appearance: the ponytail—either sleek or curled—is the cheerleader's go-to look, so if your hair is long enough, pull it all back so the judges can see your smile and facial expressions. Add a pop of color with a hair ribbon, but be sure it's tied or clipped securely so that it won't slip out mid-round-off. Short hair should be secured away from your face, too, if possible.

If you ordinarily wear makeup, then there's no reason to skip it at tryouts, unless the coach has specified that she prefers the natural look. You want your facial features to stand out, so if you're familiar with applying cosmetics, go for it. You could add a little more drama to your usual makeup routine by choosing a brightly colored lip gloss, for example, or a darker mascara.* If you've *never* worn makeup before, then tryout day is definitely not the time to experiment. The important thing is to look and feel like yourself.

Finally, make sure you know and follow the squad's policy on nail polish—some only allow clear polish—and skip jewelry completely.

* See Chapter Six, "Get the Look."

IF YOU DON'T MAKE *the* CUT

Sometimes competition is stiff or a tryout doesn't go as planned. If you don't make the squad, don't be too discouraged. There may be other cheer opportunities in your town that you hadn't considered—including classes you could take to learn skills that could catapult you among the top contenders at next year's tryout. And in the meantime, there are plenty of other ways to get involved at school and share your spirit. Here are some ideas:

MASCOTS
Many schools employ the talents of a costumed mascot to charge up the crowd. Mascots may join cheerleaders on the sidelines and often take part in cheers, dances, and halftime shows. They can also go into the stands to engage directly with fans. Inquire with the cheer coach about how to get on the short list for mascot duty.

TEAM MANAGERS
Wanted: enthusiastic, organized individuals to help communicate information to all team members, organize practice and game schedules, and keep track of and transport equipment to and from games. Some managers handle scorekeeping duties, too.

BOOSTERS OR PEP CLUB
Most schools have some version of this hardworking organization. If you join, you'll have lots of opportunities to contribute your school spirit, from making signs to selling popcorn to planning postgame receptions for team parents and alumni.

part

2

READY? OKAY!

a cheerleader's life

Congratulations! You made the squad! After you celebrate your success—with hugs all around and a visit to your favorite fro-yo shop—it's time to start planning your upcoming cheer year. Count on this: it will be packed. Though your first appearance in uniform might be months away, many squads start practicing soon after members have been chosen, and you'll want to find out any upcoming camp and competition dates as soon as possible. Also build in time for pep rallies and bonfires, sign-making, fundraising, and community service. "Cheerleading is a huge commitment," says Kia Miller, who cheered at the University of Central Florida. "You will be spending a lot of time with your squad!"

Signed, Sealed, and Delivered

Some coaches will ask you to sign a cheer contract once you make the squad. Don't worry—you won't need to secure the services of a cheer lawyer! A cheer contract is a written agreement that outlines everything that will be expected of you over the course of the season. By signing this document, you are giving your word to your coaches and the rest of the squad that you will adhere to the team rules and obligations. Your parents might be asked to "co-" or "counter-sign" so that they also know what's expected of you.

Contracts will, of course, differ from squad to squad, and they may get more detailed and complicated for more competitive, higher-profile programs, but generally speaking, they will probably cover the following topics.

★ **Attendance Requirements:** Some things, like summer camp, might be mandatory. For others, you might be excused only if you are sick or have a family emergency. Missing too many scheduled events—even practices—might lead to consequences such as having to sit out a game.

★ **A Code of Conduct:** This might be general, or it could go into detail about things such as where you can keep your cell phone during games or what kinds of photographs you can post online.

★ **Appearance and Cheer Gear:** Learn your coach's expectations about how to maintain your uniform, how to wear your hair and makeup, and any other targeted rules, such as no nail polish or jewelry.

★ **Academic Requirements:** Cheerleaders are typically expected to maintain a certain grade point average (often something in the B range).

GUYS on the SQUAD

Alot of guys get involved with cheerleading after they attend their sisters' or girlfriends' cheerleading events or competitions and think, *That looks cool!* Guys add so much to a cheering squad: loud, deep voices; intense energy; and strength. Top male cheerleaders can hold a girl above their heads with a single hand! They can power a dazzling basket toss. And many can cheer and tumble with the best of the girls.

For guys who are inclined to try it, cheerleading can be lots of fun and serve up some serious life benefits. Read what these successful guys have to say about their involvement.

RONNIE PATRICK, cheered for Morehead State University and the University of Tennessee

"I played football and did shotput in high school. Then some buddies and I decided to try all star cheerleading after watching my little sister's competition. It was challenging to learn. Nobody comes to stunting and tumbling naturally. I'm a pretty big guy, so no one could spot my gymnastics and it was hard to get over the fear of throwing a tuck, but I eventually got it. Lifting a girl in the air was a big deal—and a way to show off. I am really competitive, so I would work endless hours, practicing stunts over and over again, until I nailed them. Repetition leads to consistency.

"It's a girl-dominated sport, so guys are needed. I always say—use it to get your college paid for. If you realize you're not going to get the football or basketball or track scholarship, go to a few clinics, try out for a college squad, and if you land a scholarship, you won't need to start your life with a ton of student loan debt."

BLAKE JOHNSON, cheered for the University of Kentucky

"I played lots of sports my entire life. Even while I was an all star cheerleader during high school, I was also playing football, basketball, and baseball and running track.

"Guy cheerleaders have to be incredibly athletic. You train your muscles as if you're a football lineman, and you train your speed as if you're a track star. Once you combine those things with knowledge, it's awesome. It also helps to be an extremely outgoing person who loves to have a good time. And I really like the competitive side of cheerleading, because I love performing and putting on a show.

"Cheerleading can help you with other parts of your life, too. Because you're dealing with a lot of different women, you learn to understand them better. For example, they tend to be a little more sensitive about some things. Understanding this helps a lot when you're building a relationship."

JACOB BENEDICT, cheered for the University of Central Florida

"I was a gymnast for ten years, but stopped when I got too tall. One of my friends who was a cheerleader convinced me to go to one of her tumbling classes and the coach said I had to do cheer. I started in my senior year of high school, for my school and for an all star program.

"It's a very athletic sport, but different from most of the ones guys have done, so you have to be open to new things. It's good to be really well conditioned and strong. We do a lot of weight lifting and tumbling practice.

"You're surrounded by a bunch of beautiful girls all the time, so there's no problem with that! It's also really easy to meet people because you're a big part of the school. You immediately have something to talk about with the other students.

"The stereotype that cheerleaders are ditzy or nonathletic is totally wrong. I was premed and a biology major, so I was studying all the time! Cheerleading is a big commitment, but school came first."

The Cheer Year

One thing is sure: your life as a cheerleader will never be dull! It's typically a yearlong commitment, with something major happening almost every month. Below is a list of events and moments that take place over the course of a cheerleader's year.

PREPPING FOR PEP

★ **Tryouts** will take place at the end of the school year, sometime during the summer, or at the beginning of the school year.

★ **Practices** may be held over the summer, but often with an abbreviated schedule that allows for other obligations like swim meets or family vacations. Once school starts, your squad may practice once a week—or a lot more if you are serious about competing to win! Practice frequency and intensity can increase as you get closer to performance time—whether at a game, pep rally, special appearance, or competition.

★ **Camp** is practically a cheerleading rite of passage. Whether it's an overnight adventure or a three-day intensive held in the school gym, it's where your squad may learn many of the cheers and chants you'll perform all year long; where you will improve your jumps; and where you will be taught the proper techniques for safe stunting. It might also be where you will learn choreography for dance routines that you can perform at pep rallies, on the sidelines, at halftime, or even at competitions.

Physically, camp is about as tough as it gets. It involves long (sometimes twelve-hour-long!) days where you're pushing your cheerleading skills to the next level. You'll move from one element to the next under the instruction of experts, who are usually seasoned cheerleaders with at least college-level experience. Expect to come away from camp with sore muscles, but also with strengthened bonds with your squad and a repertoire of amazing new cheerleading feats. To find a camp that's right for your squad or even for you as an individual, go to varsity.com. There are lots of options, including these:

★ Overnight camps, when your squad heads to a specified location, usually a college campus, and stays for three or four days alongside other squads.

★ Resort camps, which combine cheerleading training with a touch of vacation. These are held at luxury hotels or dream locations and build in spare time for fun and team bonding.

★ Private or home camps, when instructors come to your town.

★ Day camps, which your squad may attend for a few days while leaving your evenings free.

★ Fall refresher camps, in case everyone took the summer off.

★ Choreography camps, where instructors will personalize a routine just for your squad.

★ Youth camps, geared to elementary or middle school cheerleaders.

★ Christian camps, which may include faith-based activities like Bible study.

★ Stunt and performance camps, which teach cheering skills like stunts, pyramids, basket tosses, and tumbling, but not cheers, chants, or routines.

★ All star camps, which focus on the stunting and tumbling skills that all star cheerleaders need.

★ Dance camp, for dance teams. These may focus on technique, offer master classes, or help choreograph and polish routines.

★ College camps, which teach the highest-level skills to university squads.

SUPPORTING THE TEAMS

★ Football

Cheerleading originated here, and remains a huge part of the gridiron scene. You'll welcome the players onto the field; fire up the crowd; and perform cheers, stunts, dances, and even tumbling on the sidelines. Your squad may also take the field as part of the halftime show. Football season tends to run from late summer through the fall, with some preseason scrimmages in the spring or early summer, and postseason matchups and championships happening in December or beyond.

★ Basketball

Cheerleaders are equally or even more prominent at basketball games. Since the court is much smaller than a football field, you'll have people on both sides watching you. You'll cheer as the team warms up, from the sidelines throughout the game, and often at center court between quarters and at halftime. Basketball starts in the fall and can run into the spring—especially if your team makes the playoffs (and with you cheering for them, of course they will!).

★ All Other Sports

Cheerleaders may be called upon to cheer for other sports as schedules allow. You might find yourself supporting the wrestlers, the soccer team—even baseball, softball, volleyball, or rowing!

UPHOLDING SCHOOL TRADITIONS

Cheerleaders have a crucial responsibility to support school traditions, especially those related to spirit. Most cheerleaders are responsible for perpetuating the spirit activities that are unique to each school. For example, at the end of the third quarter of an Indiana University football game, and at the third time-out of the school's basketball games, the cheerleaders perform the *William Tell* Overture. "Everyone knows when it's coming," says IU cheerleader Caity Hinshaw. The squad members run out onto the court carrying large flags, spell out their school name, then run back to the sidelines while the crowd chants along with the band. "It's a huge tradition," she says. Teams can also create new traditions if they don't already exist at a school. Camp is a great place to learn about creating and implementing traditions.

★ **Spirit Week**

During Spirit Week, students are encouraged to dress up (in school colors, wearing crazy hats, in semiformal attire, as what they want to be when they grow up, and so on). They may play games that pit them against other classes or grades, go on a scavenger hunt, or create window or mural designs. Cheerleaders may help organize and run the events, and might decorate the hallways, gym, or campus to get everyone super pumped up.

★ **Homecoming**

Usually held in the fall in conjunction with a football game, homecoming welcomes back alumni of the school. The celebration can include a pep rally, a parade, and the selection of a king, queen, and homecoming court, all topped off with a homecoming dance. Some schools add in their own unusual homecoming traditions. The University of Central Florida holds a "Spirit Splash" in a reflecting pond that is normally off-limits to everyone, except on this occasion, when thousands of students jump in for a swim. "The pond fills up with tons of people and we do a big performance," says former UCF cheerleader Jacob Benedict.

★ Game Days

At some schools, cheerleaders may wear their uniforms to class on game days. Players might sport their football jerseys or basketball warm-ups. And for major contests—against your biggest rival, or for a championship game—you might go all out by throwing a pep rally, papering the school with signs, or decorating players' homes with streamers, balloons, Silly String, and even more signs. Cheerleaders from the University of Tennessee head down to the local supermarket in the hours before a football game to perform cheers right next to the checkout aisles! In exchange for spreading school spirit to the locals, they take back trays of snacks to munch on during halftime and to share with the opposing team's cheerleaders.

Proving Your Prowess

Some squads, including those from STUNT and all star programs, focus solely on competing pure cheerleading skills. But most other squads add cheerleading competitions or contests to everything else they do. That means many cheerleaders are squeezing in practices for competitions, which are often held in early winter, between basketball games and holiday plans.

Competition season starts at the regional level in the fall, when organizations like Varsity host events all over the United States. Nationals season starts after the new year, giving squads the chance to compete against the nation's best.

Here's where cheerleading can really get intense! Some squads practice up to fifteen hours per week to ensure they perform their absolute best when it's their turn out on the mat.

ROCKING IT *at* COMPETITIONS

The lights are bright, the arena is large, and the other teams are impressive! Still, there are ways to make sure your squad stands out when it's your turn to take the floor. Josh McCurdy, UCA's Director of Curriculum and a longtime cheerleading judge, offers these tips.

FOLLOW THE RULES

Make sure you are following all the regulations—from the length of the routine, to what kinds of cheer elements you can use, to how many stunts you can put up at one time (usually based on the size of your squad). And take note of year-to-year rule changes. These might allow you to add something new to your routine.

KNOW THE SCORE

Try to get your hands on a score sheet in advance. "It will tell you what a judge is looking for in a routine," says Josh. It might be something like twenty points for stunts, compared to five for jumps, so you'll know where to focus your efforts in practice.

BE REAL

You want to look like you're doing a cheer at a game and getting people to yell with you. "Look natural, have a lot of energy, and don't be so robotic," says Josh. There *is* such a thing as "too choreographed." Just go out there and smile and have a lot of fun. "The judges will remember that and will tend to score you better because they are liking your energy," he says.

CUT THE DISTRACTIONS

Avoid the following: a rushed routine that looks panicked. Transitions where people move all the way from one side of the mat to the other. Obnoxious facial expressions, like blowing kisses or winking. A crazy-colored uniform or tall leopard-print socks. Huge floppy bows. "You don't want the judges to remember something like that instead of something good in your routine," says Josh.

HIT YOUR ROUTINE

Top cheerleading routines push the limit, and stunts sometimes fall: everyone knows that. But for your best chance at a top score, perform the hardest routine you think you can do perfectly because you've done it so many times in practice. "The performance should not be the first time you hit your routine," says Josh.

BRING SOMETHING NEW

"Any time you're doing something that people have never seen, you'll wow the judges," says Josh. It could be a creative stunt sequence or really elite tumbling—maybe even a dance move you invented yourselves!

DON'T FORGET THE BASICS!

"A lot of times," says Josh, "squads will put up a nice stunt, but when they hit the high V, it's not sharp." The topping finishes the stunt and makes it look nice, so never forget about being sharp with your motions. Polish little things like that in every practice so that you'll be confident when it's time to go out onto the mat.

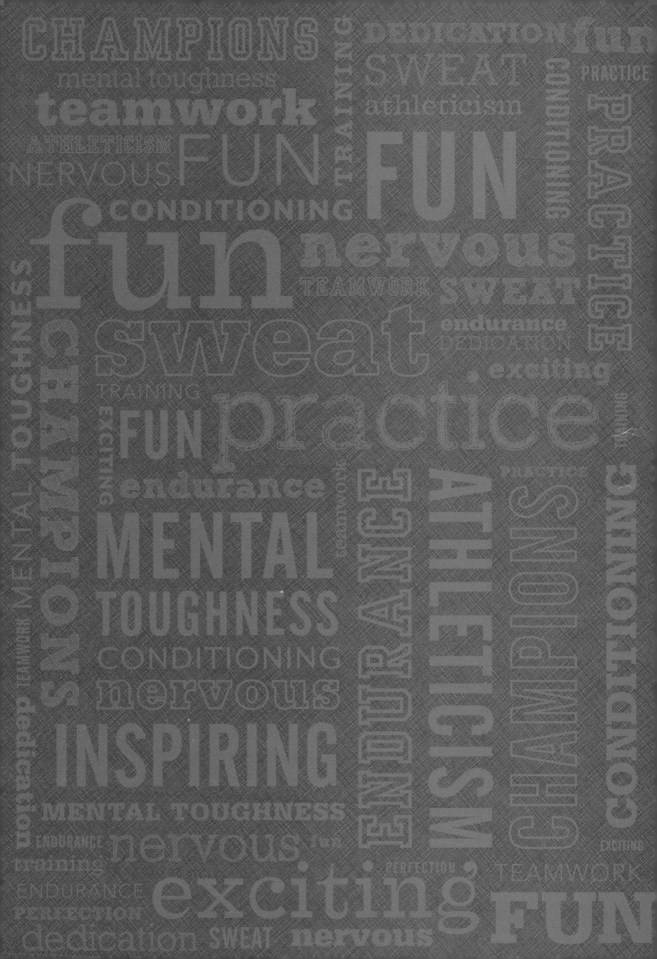

all *the* right moves

One of the most exciting parts of being a cheerleader is performing the incredible athletic feats that make the crowd go wild. Pristine, perfectly timed jumps, fantastic tumbling, gravity-defying pyramids, and flawless basket tosses are all great ways to dazzle the fans.

In this section, you'll learn about some tried-and-true cheerleading jumps and stunts, broken down into step-by-step instructions. You'll also get a refresher on the basic elements of some of the most recognized cheer motions. Of course, reviewing this section is no substitute for being taught and coached by a professional instructor at camp. Camp is where you learn all the fundamentals of cheerleading.

Think of these next few pages as a primer, or a jumping-off point (literally!), for learning the skills every cheerleader needs to know. By studying these photos and descriptions, you'll begin to familiarize yourself with the elements of jumps and stunting.

PLAY IT SAFE

Like almost everything else in life, cheerleading involves a certain degree of risk. You will be doing difficult stunts and tumbling, and there's a chance that someone could get hurt. Bumps, bruises, and ankle and wrist sprains are the most common injuries. To minimize the risk of injury, you should act responsibly at all times.

As the leader in the cheerleading community, Varsity has worked hard to ensure that cheerleading is safe for everyone. Your coaches should be able to teach you the best ways to lower the risk of injury, but if you'd like to study up on your own (which is highly recommended), a thorough list of safety guidelines and regulations is available at aacca.org.

In the meantime, these tips will help you stay safe:

★ MAKE SURE YOUR MEDICAL FORMS ARE UP TO DATE. They should include information about medications you are taking and any allergies you have. Check that all contact information for your parents and your doctor is current and accurate. Your coach should have this data handy at all times—at practices, competitions, and games (both home and away).

★ ONLY DO YOUR ROUTINES—ESPECIALLY THE MORE DIFFICULT STUNTING OR TUMBLING—IF YOU'RE 100 PERCENT UP FOR IT. This means you should be properly trained, warmed up, and feeling good. If you're not feeling healthy, if something hurts (like your head or your wrist), or if you are overly tired or very upset about something, tell your coaches. They'll decide the best way to go forward.

★ PRACTICE IS NOT THE PLACE FOR GOOFING AROUND OR BEING SILLY. Try to schedule your practices in a place where there will be no distractions. Focus and remain serious.

★ MAKE SURE YOUR PRACTICE AND CHEER ENVIRONMENT IS SUITABLE FOR WHAT YOU'RE DOING. The area should be well lit and spacious. And if you're learning something new, you should be on an appropriate surface. Clear the floor before you practice or perform—make sure no one has left a cheer bag or warm-up jacket lying around where someone could trip over it.

★ **KNOW YOUR LIMITS.** This means never attempting something you haven't yet been properly trained to execute. Cheer skills follow a progression; you begin with simple basics and increase the difficulty of the moves as you go. Be patient. With proper training, you'll be able to perform stunts and skills to the best of your ability.

★ **DRESS PROPERLY.** This means no overly baggy clothing. Always wear approved, securely tied cheer shoes, and no jewelry.

★ **STUNT SAFELY.** Bases and back spots should keep their focus on the girl who's up in the air, and she, in turn, should do her best to keep her balance and hit her positions.

★ **IF YOU HAVE CONCERNS ABOUT SAFETY—YOURS OR ANYONE ELSE'S—SPEAK UP.** Maybe you're feeling pressured by teammates to perform a skill you aren't comfortable doing. Or you notice someone doing something incorrectly that could lead to injury. Raise your concerns politely but firmly. Speaking up could help keep everyone on your squad safe and is part of true teamwork.

★ **HAVE A PLAN IN PLACE IN CASE SOMEONE DOES GET HURT.** Everyone should stay calm while the coach or trainer checks the injury. A designated person—perhaps the captain—should call 911 if necessary, while the coach remains with the injured teammate.

Jumps

Jumps are performed to create excitement, to get the crowd's attention, and to display athleticism. It is important always to use correct technique when performing jumps. Below are a few jumps to get you started. Each begins with a three-step approach:

THE APPROACH

1. Clasp your hands.

2. Hit a high V.

3. Start your jump by bending your knees and crossing your arms in front of you.

TOE TOUCH

Jump off the ground as high as you can while lifting your arms into a T and lifting your chest up. Try to open your hips and focus on bringing your legs up to your arms, not the other way around!

FRONT HURDLER

Jump off the ground as high as you can while lifting your arms into a touchdown motion. Bring your right leg up to your chest and bend your left leg back behind you. This jump can be performed on either side.

PIKE

Jump off the ground as high as you can and bring your arms around to hit candlesticks. Squeeze your legs together and bring them up parallel with your arms.

JUMP EXERCISES

Jumps are a big part of what cheerleaders do to help create excitement on the sidelines. These jump exercises will help you improve your flexibility and strength.

LUNGES

1. *Start with your feet together.*

2. *Step forward with one leg; bend both knees until they are both close to ninety-degree angles. Make sure your front knee is directly above your ankle; make sure your other knee doesn't touch the floor. Push back to the starting position and repeat on the other leg.*

SITTING TOE TOUCH

1. *Lie flat on your back, feet together and arms near your ears.*

2. *Using your core, bring your upper body up while bringing your toes up and out, hitting a "seated toe touch" position.*

3. *Slowly lower yourself back down. Concentrate on keeping your legs straight and toes pointed. Repeat exercise at least five times.*

SEATED STRADDLE LIFT

1. Start in a straddle position with your hands on both sides of your leg at about your knee.

2. Lift your leg, working your hip flexor muscles. Make sure you do not lean over.
Try to stay sitting up as straight as possible.

3. Repeat on your other leg.

4. Place both hands in front of you, about six inches from your body.

5. Lift both legs at the same time, using both of your hip flexor muscles.

Stunts

Stunts were designed to grab the crowd's attention, to help lead the crowd, and to show athleticism. Proper stunt technique is learned at the beginning of the season at summer camp. When learning new skills, follow the proper stunt progressions.

AN IMPORTANT NOTE: All cheerleading skills, including partner stunts such as the ones listed below, should be performed under the supervision of a knowledgeable adult.

WHO'S WHO: STUNT POSITIONS

★ **Back spot:** a person who is responsible for assisting and catching the top person in a partner stunt and/or pyramid

★ **Base (main/secondary):** the bottom person of a partner stunt and/or pyramid

★ **Top:** the top person of a partner stunt and/or pyramid

1/2 UP TO SWEDISH FALLS

1.

Main base: *Stand slightly to the left side of the top and grab her under her arms.*

Secondary base: *Grab the top's right toe with your left hand and grab her calf with your right hand.*

Back spot: *Grab the top's waist with both hands.*

Top: *With your body facing the side, offer your right foot up to the secondary base and place your hands on the main base's shoulders.*

2.

3.

Main base: *Straighten your arms as the top jumps from the ground.*

Secondary base: *Follow the top as she jumps off the ground. Start to drive up with your right hand. Her leg will turn in your hands so that her knee is facing down.*

Back spot: *Follow the top as she jumps off the ground. Start to step closer to the stunt so you can help support the top.*

Top: *Jump off your left leg and put your weight in your arms.*

Main base: *Lock out your arms. Your shoulders should be directly under the top's shoulders.*

Secondary base: *Lock out your arms and regrab the top's thigh with your right hand.*

Back spot: *Step closer to the stunt and continue to help support the top.*

Top: *Keep your arms and legs locked out. Lift your left leg up in the air and point your toe.*

All: *To dismount, the top puts her leg down and all others rotate back to the starting position.*

 # HANG DRILL

Before performing the extension prep stunt, be sure that you and your teammates can successfully perform this hang drill.

★ BASES: Face each other with your legs slightly bent. Hold the top's feet when she jumps into the load position. Once the top is holding her weight in her arms, you may release her feet to test her strength and ability to hold the load position.

★ TOP: Place your arms on the shoulders of the bases and then jump so that you are supporting your weight in your arms. Your legs should be bent, and you should not be supporting your weight with your feet.

★ BACK SPOT: Start by holding the top's waist and lift to assist her into the hang drill position. Once the top is in position, hold her ankles until the bases release her feet to test her strength.

To start this stunt, the bases stand across from each other with their knees slightly bent and their backs straight. The back spot has her hands on the top's waist, and the top has her hands on the bases' shoulders.

1.

2.

Main base: *Once the top jumps into the load position, grab her right foot with your hands. Keep your arms bent and your elbows close to your sides.*

Secondary base: *Once the top jumps into the load position, grab her left foot with your hands. Keep your arms bent and your elbows close to your sides.*

Back spot: *Once the top jumps into the load position, grab both of her ankles.*

Top: *Place your hands on your bases' shoulders and then jump into the load position. Bend your knees up toward your chest and keep all your weight in your arms.*

Main base: *Keep your arms bent and close to your sides as you dip by bending your legs. Shrug up quickly through your shoulders and start to lift the top straight up to eye level. Then settle her foot back down at chest level.*

Secondary base: *Keep your arms bent and close to your sides as you dip with your legs. Shrug up quickly through your shoulders and start to lift the top straight up to eye level. Then settle her foot back down at chest level.*

Back spot: *Dip with the bases and lift the top girl up by the ankles to chest level.*

Top: *Keep your weight in your arms as the bases dip. Then stand straight up while pulling up through your shoulders and locking out your legs and squeezing them close together. Hit a high V.*

1.

2.

3.

Main base: *Once the top jumps into the load position, grab her right foot with your hands. Keep your arms bent and your elbows close to your sides.*

Secondary base: *Once the top jumps into the load position, grab her left foot with your hands. Keep your arms bent and your elbows close to your sides.*

Back spot: *Once the top jumps into the load position, grab both of her ankles.*

Top: *Place your hands on your bases' shoulders and then jump into the load position. Bend your knees up toward your chest and keep all your weight in your arms.*

Main base: *Keep your arms bent and close to your sides as you dip by bending your legs. Shrug up quickly through your shoulders and start to lift the top straight up to eye level. Then settle her foot back down to chest level.*

Secondary base: *Keep your arms bent and close to your sides as you dip with your legs. Shrug up quickly through your shoulders and start to lift the top straight up to eye level. Then settle her foot back down to chest level.*

Back spot: *Dip with the bases and lift the top by the ankles up to chest level. Always look at the top.*

Top: *Keep your weight in your arms as the bases dip. Then stand straight up while locking out your legs and squeezing them close together. Hit a high V.*

Main base: *Bend your knees and drive your arms up while looking up at the top. Lock out your arms and legs.*

Secondary base: *Bend your knees and drive your arms up while looking up at the top. Lock out your arms and legs.*

Back spot: *Dip with the bases and keep your hands on the top's ankles as you help drive the stunt up. Be sure to look at the top.*

Top: *Keep your legs locked out and continue squeezing them together. Once you have reached the top, hit a high V.*

Before performing this stunt, be sure you have successfully done a press extension.

1.

2.

Main base: *Once the top jumps into load position, grab her right foot with your hands. Keep your arms bent and your elbows close to your sides.*

Secondary base: *Once the top jumps into the load position, grab her left foot with your hands. Keep your arms bent and your elbows close to your sides.*

Back spot: *Once the top jumps into the load position, grab both of her ankles.*

Top: *Place your hands on your bases' shoulders and then jump into load position. Bend your knees up toward your chest and keep all your weight in your arms.*

Main base: *Keep your arms bent and close to your sides as you dip by bending your legs. Shrug up quickly through your shoulders and start to lift the top straight up by locking out your arms and legs.*

Secondary base: *Keep your arms bent and close to your sides as you dip with your legs. Shrug up quickly through your shoulders and start to lift the top straight up by locking out your arms and legs.*

Back spot: *Stay on the top's ankles the entire time as you help drive the stunt up. Keep looking at the top.*

Top: *Keep your weight in your arms as the bases dip. Then stand straight up while locking out your legs and squeezing them close together. Once you have reached the top, hit a high V.*

To start this stunt, the top faces the main base.

1.

2.

Main base: *Grab the top's right heel with your left hand and stack your right hand under your left hand or place it under the toe. Bend low so that the top can easily stand up over you while you keep your back straight.*

Secondary base: *Start by facing the top's back and grab her waist.*

Back spot: *Start with your right hand on the top's right ankle and your left hand underneath the seat.*

Top: *Offer the main base your right foot and grab the secondary base's wrists.*

Main base: *Follow the top as she dips with her legs and starts to stand up. Stand up quickly. Keep your left hand on the top's heel and move your right hand around to grab the top's toe. Take the stunt slightly above eye level before settling back down to the extension prep.*

Secondary base: *Follow the top as she dips with her legs and starts to stand up. Stand up quickly. At the top of the stunt, release her waist and then spot for her left foot. Grab her left foot as soon as you can.*

Back spot: *Follow the top as she dips with her legs and starts to stand up. Stand up quickly so that you can drive up through the seat while lifting up on the right ankle. Keep your right hand on the top's right ankle, and then grab the top's left ankle with your left hand and continue to lift up.*

Top: *Dip with your legs and think about standing up over the main base by putting all your weight in your right leg. Lock out both legs and continue to squeeze them together. Don't try to guide your left foot to the secondary base or to spin yourself to the front. Hit a high V when you are at the top of the stunt.*

3.

Once you have mastered the 1/4 up extension prep, you can progress to a 1/4 up extension.

Main base: *Keep your left hand on the top's heel and move your right hand around to grab the top's toes as you drive to the top of the stunt. Keep shrugging up through your shoulders while locking out your arms.*

Secondary base: *After releasing the top girl's waist at the top of the stunt, leave your hands open and spot for the left foot. Grab it as soon as you can and lock out your arms while bending at your knees to absorb the weight.*

Back spot: *Stay on the top's right ankle with your right hand as you finish through to the extension with your left hand. Grab the left ankle with your left hand and keep lifting up.*

Top: *Dip with your legs and think about standing up over the main base by putting all your weight in your right leg. Lock out both legs and continue to squeeze them together. Don't try to guide your left foot to the secondary base or to spin yourself to the front. Hit a high V when you are at the top of the stunt.*

These directions are for the top's left foot behind, but you can spin either way. Even though the top is facing a different direction, the bases and back spot will stay facing the same way.

1.

2.

Main base: *Stack your left hand on top of your right hand and grab only the heel of the top's right foot when she jumps into the load position.*

Secondary base: *Stack your left hand on top of your right hand and grab only the toe of the top's left foot when she jumps into the load position.*

Back spot: *Don't cross your arms. Once the top has jumped into the load position, grab her right ankle with your right hand and her left ankle with your left hand.*

Top: *Start by facing the bases with your back to the crowd. Jump into the load position with your left leg crossed behind your right. Keep all your weight in your arms, none in your feet. You can stop in this position to make sure everyone has the correct grip.*

Main base: *Dip with your legs as you would for a regular extension prep. Shrug up through your shoulders and focus on taking the stunt up before you think about spinning. Once the stunt is at eye level, start to unwind your hands to grab the top's toes with your right hand while keeping a grip with your left hand.*

Secondary base: *Dip with your legs as you would for a regular extension prep. Shrug up through your shoulders and focus on taking the stunt up before you think about spinning. Once the stunt is at eye level, start to unwind your hands to grab the top's heel with your right hand while keeping a grip with your left hand.*

Back spot: *Dip together with the bases and think about driving up to the top as in a regular extension prep, lifting up on the top's ankles. Continue to lift while you help to uncross the top's ankles once the stunt is at eye level. Help to keep the top's feet close together.*

Top: *Wait for the bases to dip; then think about standing straight up as you would for a regular extension prep. Don't try to spin your body. Instead, stand up straight and squeeze your legs together—this will help create the spin.*

3.

Main base: *Once you have your regular extension prep grip and the stunt is at eye level, settle into the extension prep position.*

Secondary base: *Once you have your regular extension prep grip and the stunt is at eye level, settle into the extension prep position.*

Back spot: *Continue lifting up on the top's ankles the entire time.*

Top: *Once you have spun to the front, continue lifting through your shoulders and squeezing your legs together. Hit a high V.*

4.

Once you have mastered the 1/2 up extension prep, you can progress to a 1/2 up extension.

Main base: *Once you have your regular grip, continue shrugging up through your shoulders. Always catch with your arms locked out.*

Secondary base: *Once you have your regular grip, continue shrugging up through your shoulders. Always catch with your arms locked out.*

Back spot: *Continue lifting up on the top's ankles the entire time.*

Top: *Once you have spun to the front, continue lifting through your shoulders and squeezing your legs together. Hit a high V.*

Before performing this stunt, be sure you have successfully done an extension.

1.

All: *This stunt should start with the top jumping into a regular load position. Take one dip together as a group.*

2.

Main base: *After the group dip, bend at your knees and stay at the load position.*

Secondary base: *After the group dip, stand up and lift the top's left foot up to the extension prep level.*

Back spot: *After the group dip, guide the top's ankles while lifting the top's left leg up to an extension prep and keeping the top's right leg in the load position.*

Top: *After the group dip, lift your left leg up to an extension prep. Make sure you are still lifting through your shoulders and keeping your hips underneath you.*

Main base: *Dip and then drive the top's right foot all the way up to an extension by using your legs and arms. Absorb the weight by bending with your legs.*

Secondary base: *Stay at the extension prep level.*

Back spot: *Keep lifting up on both ankles while driving the top's right foot all the way to the top and keeping the top's left foot at the extension prep level.*

Top: *Lock out your left leg and lift your right leg up to an extension. Keep lifting up through your shoulders and staying tight.*

Main base: *Stay in an extension while the secondary base drives the top's left foot up to meet you in an extension.*

Secondary base: *Dip and then drive all the way up to an extension.*

Back spot: *Drive the top's left leg up to meet her right leg.*

Top: *Stand up on your right leg and squeeze your legs together. Hit a high V.*

Before performing this stunt, be sure you have successfully done an extension.

1.

2.

3.

Main base: *Start with a slight bend in your knees and your arms ready to grab the top's foot as she walks in.*

Secondary base: *Start with a slight bend in your knees and your arms ready to grab the top's foot as she walks in.*

Back spot: *Start on the right side of the top so that you can follow her as she walks in.*

Top: *Start about one step away from the bases.*

Main base: *As the top walks in, grab her right foot with both of your hands as you would for an extension.*

Secondary base: *As the top walks in, grab the liberty grip on her right foot. Place your right hand under the top's foot and between the main base's hands. Place your left hand on the main base's right wrist as if you are looking at a watch.*

Back spot: *Follow the top as she walks into the load position. Grab her right ankle with your right hand and place your left hand under the seat.*

Top: *Step with your left foot and then place your right foot into the load while putting all of your weight in your arms.*

Main and secondary bases: *Dip by bending your legs so that the top taps the ground.*

Back spot: *Dip by bending your legs so that the top taps the ground.*

Top: *Tap the ground with your left foot while supporting your weight with your arms.*

4.

Main and secondary bases: *Stand up quickly and lock your arms and legs to drive the stunt up. Keep pushing the stunt up in the liberty grip with your arms locked out.*

Back spot: *Stand up quickly, pushing through the seat and lifting up on the top's right ankle. Then grab the top's right ankle with both hands.*

Top: *Stand up quickly, pushing through your arms and locking out your leg. Keep all your weight on your right leg and squeeze your left foot to your right knee. Hit a high V and keep lifting up through your shoulders and squeezing your core.*

VARIATIONS ON STEP 4: After mastering the liberty, the top may also perform heel stretch and arabesque body positions. The top should master these positions on the ground before attempting them in a group stunt.

Heel Stretch: *Start with your arms in a high V. Keep your right leg locked and bring your left leg up to your left hand and grab the middle of your left foot. The palm of your hand should be on the outside of your shoe. Be sure your leg does not go out to the side, and keep your chest up. Your arms should resemble a high V, except your left arm will be holding your left foot.*

Arabesque: *Extend your arms in a T motion. Lift your left leg up behind you. Your leg should be parallel to the ground or higher. Be sure not to drop your chest. Once you have hit the arabesque, turn your head to the front.*

MASTERING *the* LIBERTY GRIP

This is the most common grip.

★ **MAIN BASE:** Grab the top's foot. Your right hand should have a firm grip under the front of the foot, and your left hand should provide a strong foundation for the heel. Once the stunt reaches the top, lock your arms so that your body is in a straight line.

★ **SECONDARY BASE:** Grip the middle of the top's foot with your right hand. Raise your left hand, look at the top of your wrist (as if you were looking at a watch), and grab the top of the main base's front wrist. Use this positioning to help pull up on the stunt. Once the stunt reaches the top, lock your arms so that your body is in a straight line.

★ **BACK SPOT:** Grab the top's ankle with your right hand and lift up. Once the stunt reaches the top, continue to pull up the entire time. If you are not tall enough to grab the ankle, hold on to the bases' wrists instead.

The BUMP DOWN

The bump down is a simple way to dismount from group skills.

STEP 1

Main base: From the extension prep, dip by bending your knees and drive your hands up to slightly above eye level.

Secondary base: From the extension prep, dip by bending your knees and drive your hands up to slightly above eye level.

Back spot: From the extension prep, continue to pull up on the top's ankles, keeping her feet close together.

Top: Stay in the extension prep, keeping your core tight and feet close together.

STEP 2

Main base: Return to the load position, keeping your arms bent and your elbows close to your sides. Release to allow the top's feet to land on the ground.

Secondary base: Return to the load position, keeping your arms bent and your elbows close to your sides.

Back spot: Stay with the top's ankles and return to the load position. Release quickly to allow the top's feet to land on the ground.

Top: As the bases return to the load position, slightly bend your knees to return to the load position. Make sure you bend your knees up toward your chest and support all your weight with your arms. When the bases release your feet, keep weight in your arms until your feet land on the ground.

Say It Loud

Cheerleading started more than one hundred years ago with yells, chants, and cheers that pulled in the crowd, and this is still a huge part of your work. Most of your game-day cheering will take place on the sidelines and consist of arm motions and cheers. Some of your words are specific to what's actually happening in the sporting event. For example, at football games there are cheers to support the defensive players ("PUSH 'EM BACK!") or to encourage a gain of yards ("OFFENSE, MOVE THAT BALL!"). At basketball games you'll be chanting for "TWO POINTS MORE!" or yelling for a rebound. Here's how to make yourself heard.

PROJECT YOUR VOICE

Your cheerleading voice should be deeper, and much louder, than your ordinary voice. The power comes from your diaphragm, which is just below your breastbone. Using your diaphragm creates a stronger voice in a lower octave that will carry farther and resonate more. Avoid shouting from your throat, which sounds more shrill and screechy and can result in your losing your voice.

EMPHASIZE THE RIGHT SYLLABLES

The way to cheer in unison as a squad is to know when to pause, when to lengthen or clip off a word, and when to shout as loud as you can. This produces the deliberate rhythm that distinguishes cheerleading from other kinds of vocal expression. You need to practice cheers and chants in advance so that you know how your squad performs them. If you aren't 100 percent sure, let your captains take the lead; turn up your volume once you've figured it out. You want to put special emphasis on the words that you want the crowd to yell with you.

ARTICULATE THE WORDS

Don't run your words together. It sounds sloppy and takes away from the message you're hoping to relay. Instead, clearly pronounce and finish each word—for example, giving a little extra oomph to the *T* at the end of "FIGHT!"

KEEP 'EM CLEAN

Some chants will use the name of the opposing team ("WATCH OUT, BULLDOGS!"), but remember never to use words or phrases that are negative or insulting. Cheers should always be upbeat, positive, and sportsmanlike. It's fine to assure the fans that "WE'RE GONNA BEAT STATE," but you should never say anything that belittles or degrades your opponents. Keep it friendly and classy.

Add Motions

Motions are the easiest and most effective way for a squad to lead a crowd. Incorporate the four *P*s of motion technique into your practices to perfect your motions and get them ready to lead fans on game days.

★ **Placement:** Each motion should be sharp and precise. Practice with a partner or in front of a mirror. Your arms should be locked without hyperextending elbows, and your wrists should be straight in line with your arms.

★ **Perfection:** Once you've mastered the placement of each motion, practice motion drills to beats or music to develop muscle memory for every motion. Be sure to practice both sides of any motion that is performed with one arm. You don't want to have a strong right punch and weak left punch.

★ **Precision:** When practicing with your team, practice the same motion at a fairly slow pace. Make sure everyone is hitting the motion at the same time and with the same placement.

★ **Performing:** Sharp motions greatly improve a team's performance, so it's important to spend time during practices going over everyone's technique and placement of motions. When you're comfortable and confident in your motions, you can lead a crowd at a game and breeze through motion sequences at competitions.

Popular Motions to Master

Here are some basic motions to get you started:

84

Right Half Low V

Left Half Low V

Touchdown

Broken T

Clap

Clasp

Putting It All Together

You can create your own original cheer or sideline by using different combinations of motions and adding words. Here are three simple sidelines to get you started. You can repeat sidelines as many times as you want. They should be easy for your crowd to follow!

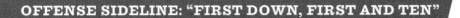

1.

Yell **"FIRST!"**
Hit a right broken T.

2.

Yell **"DOWN!"**
Step your right foot out and push your right arm across your body.

3.

Clap twice.

4.

Yell **"FIRST AND!"**
Hit a left half low V.

5.

Yell **"TEN!"**
Hit a left half high V.

1.

Yell "D!"
Stand with your feet apart and hit a right half low V.

2.

Yell "D!"
Switch to the other side.

3.

Yell "D!"
Hit a high V.

4.

Yell "D-E!"
Bend your right arm straight back.

5.

Yell "FENSE!"
Hit a right punch.

GENERAL SIDELINE: "LET'S GO TIGERS!"

1.

Yell **"LET'S!"**

Start running with your right foot forward and swing your arms.

2.

Yell **"GO!"**

Switch legs and swing your arms toward the front.

3.

Yell **"TIG!"**

Bring your feet together with a slight bend in your knees.

4.

Yell **"ERS!"**

Straighten out your legs and hit a right punch.

JUST DANCE

I f you're more interested in artistic movement than impressive stunts but still want to show your spirit, consider joining the dance team—or starting one if your school doesn't have one yet!

"It's about getting sixteen individuals to dance like one person," explains Carsen Rowe, who has been involved with dance since she was a child. She became a Crimson Girl at Washington State University and then transferred to the University of Cincinnati, where she joined the dance team. "It's incredibly challenging but so rewarding."

Many dance teams perform alongside the cheer squad on the sidelines at sporting events and perform at center court (or field) during halftime. "We do fundraisers and community service. Pretty much anything the cheer squad does, dance does, too. We're all part of the spirit squad," says Carsen.

The training of a dancer, though, is decidedly different. Carsen, for example, started in ballet, then trained in tap, jazz, and musical theater. As she got older, she added in contemporary and hip-hop. A dancer should train as much as he or she can in all sorts of styles, to become well rounded. "Look for any chance to take a class from someone new, so you can hear what they have to say about that particular style," she says.

A dance team's routine is also different from a cheer routine. "The biggest difference is that we don't stunt and we don't tumble," explains Carsen. "But we do lots of leaps, turns, lifts, and hip-hop tricks. Things are always changing and evolving, with new tricks, new turns, and new ways to create a routine. It's so artistic." Unlike the cheer squad, dance teams rarely shout, and aren't looking for crowd interaction. "The interaction is more with your body," she says.

Dance teams learn a variety of routines to compete in different categories. Pom is most like cheer, with classic positions like high Vs and low Vs mixed with leaps and pirouettes. Jazz routines can be slow and lyrical or up-tempo and sassy. Hip-hop performances incorporate many different kinds of tricks, such as front and back walkovers, handstands, head springs, and kip-ups.

Dance teams may also attend camps and compete all the way up to Nationals. "You can never be perfect, so you're always striving to be better," says Carsen. "It's always a challenge and I love that."

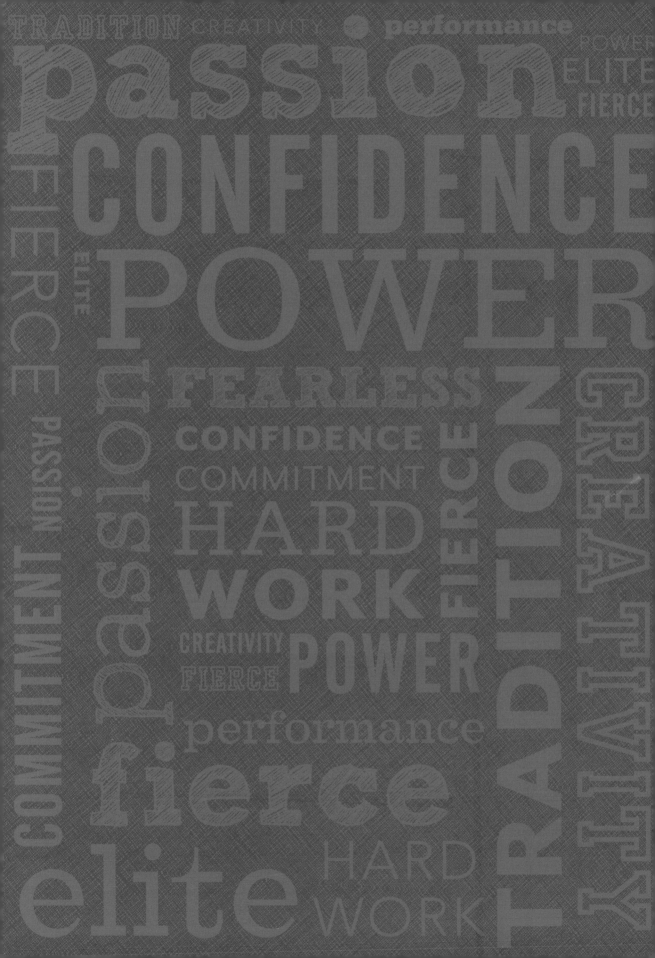

get *the* look

It's not just a colorful uniform that tells the world you're a cheerleader. Pulled-back hair and a fresh face complete the look. Here are some fail-safe hair, makeup, and clothing tips that will take you from an afternoon selling raffle tickets to raise money for new warm-ups to a Friday night football game to a national competition.

Tame Your Tresses

If your hair is chin-length or longer, the ponytail should be your go-to hairstyle for all things cheer—practices, games, pep rallies, competitions, and appearances. Long, flowing hair is great while you're sitting in class or hanging out with friends, but if it's falling in your face during your cheer routine, it will look messy and could even cause visibility problems. You don't need any hair distractions while you're performing—you have enough to think about! So here's how you can make sure it's all tied back.

THE BASIC PONYTAIL

1. Start with detangled hair and a strong elastic (ponytail holder) on your wrist.

2. Brush all your hair toward the spot where you want your ponytail to be—it can be high or low. If high, you can flip all your hair forward and brush it into a ponytail while upside down.

3. Gather all your hair into a ponytail using the hand that has the elastic on it.

4. Check it out in the mirror (flip right-side up now if you were doing this upside down). Got bumps? Smooth them out with your brush until they're gone.

5. Use your other hand to pull the elastic over the ponytail and pull hair through.

6. Twist the elastic and repeat—pull it over the ponytail and pull hair through.

7. Use your brush, comb, or fingers to smooth out any remaining bumps.

8. If you have flyaways or tendrils falling out of the ponytail, use bobby pins, small barrettes, or hair spray to secure them.

STYLE TIPS

Depending on what your squad allows (or requires), you can curl, wave, braid, straighten, or slick back the hair in your ponytail. Or add a simple ribbon to match your uniform. Be careful about getting too showy with your hair accessories, though. A giant curly bow à la Minnie Mouse might be distracting for the judges or fans who are watching you perform.

SHORT HAIR

Even short hair can interrupt your focus if it's flying in front of your face, sticking to your lip gloss or falling into your eyes. For shorter styles, smaller clip-in bows, barrettes, and elasticized, non-slip headbands can help keep your hair looking great and staying in place.

ADD SOME VOLUME

For a more dramatic look, some squads have embraced the pouf-and-ponytail combo—often topped with an attention-grabbing hair bow. Here's how to get the perfect poufy ponytail look, which works best on medium-length or long hair.

You will need a comb or brush, a hair elastic, bobby pins, and your cheer bow.

1. Brush out your hair so that it's smooth and tangle-free. Gather a three-inch-thick section at the front, as wide as your eyebrows.

2. Hold this section of hair straight up and tease it from behind. Spray with hair spray for lasting hold.

3. Flip section toward the back of your head, smoothing out the top layer with your comb or brush, and push it forward a bit to create the pouf just above your forehead. Secure in place with a few bobby pins.

4. Sweep your remaining hair into a high ponytail. Add more bobby pins to tame any flyaways. Then add a great bow!

LEAVE SOME DOWN

Some squads require ponytails at all times, but others will let you wear your hair partly down, especially if you're cheering at a frigid late-fall football game. And there are college teams that go for this look year-round.

The half-up hairstyle is a great way to show off long, pretty hair *and* keep it out of your face. For a poufier look, just follow the instructions above but leave the back half of your hair down. Or for a non-poufy version, simply smooth back the front half of your hair, secure with an elastic or reliable barrette, and add a cheer ribbon.

Game Face

For game days and competitions, most squads go for a natural look, with just enough makeup to enhance a cheerleader's features without looking extreme. The rules for makeup can differ greatly by age, with elementary school girls allowed nothing beyond colorless lip balm, while college girls sometimes must wear mascara and red lipstick. Check in with your coach or captain about what's expected of you.

If you do wear makeup, invest in waterproof or long-wearing varieties for a few good reasons:

★ **Stain Watch:** You don't want your shimmer eye shadow to leave a huge smear on your uniform.

★ **Water, Water, Everywhere:** The skies might open up while you're on the sidelines of a football game. Or you might be cheering so hard that you work up a serious sweat. Waterproof makeup will help you avoid the streaky look.

★ **Long Days:** A cheerleader's duties can last for eight or more hours at a stretch, so your makeup needs to be able to handle as much as you can.

QUICK TIP

Tuck a pocket-sized stain-remover stick or packets of individually wrapped laundry wipes in your cheer bag to keep your uniform free of makeup (and dirt/soda/mustard) at games and competitions. Also, bring a travel pack of tissues or makeup-remover wipes to deal with mascara, blush, or foundation failure.

MAKEUP 101

If your squad does allow makeup, a light application is the best way to look great and feel confident. Here, Varsity's expert makeup artist Angela Angel shares her quick routine for the perfect game-day look. Angela creates similar looks for the Varsity Spirit Fashion catalog and fashion shows.

Start with a clean face.

Use a wide brush to apply lightweight foundation, tinted moisturizer, or powder foundation.

Apply blush to the "apples" of your cheeks. Your blush color should match the natural color of your cheeks when they are flushed from exercise or from being out in the cold.

Apply eyeliner close to your upper lash line. We like cream or gel eyeliner applied with a clean eyeliner brush.

Use an eye shadow brush to apply a neutral-colored eye shadow across your entire eyelid. Chose a shade with a slight shimmer for added drama.

Apply a neutral-colored lip gloss to moisturized lips. We like using a small lip brush for extra control.

Smile!

Suit Up

Nothing beats the thrill of wearing a cheerleading uniform for the first time. Your leaders—the coach and possibly the captains—should make sure everyone gets the right size on uniform-distribution day, which will take place sometime between tryouts and your first official appearance. Try it on right away to be sure everything fits.

Once you take your uniform home, take care of it by hanging it carefully in your closet and laundering it according to the instructions, so that it's always clean and not wrinkled. Keep your socks and briefs where you can find them fast. And always check that your cheer shoes have no mud or scuffs; the laces, which are machine-washable, should be dirt-free, too.

Your uniform and cheer accessories should consist of the following items:

★ **Shell**

★ **Bodysuit**

★ **Skirt (pants for guys)**

★ **Briefs**

★ **Socks**

★ **Shoes**

★ **Hair ribbons**

★ **Team jackets**

★ **Warm-ups/sweats**

★ **Megaphone**

★ **Poms**

★ **Spirit signs**

YOU'VE GOT THIS *in the* BAG

What to Pack for Games and Competitions

If you're traveling to a far-off competition or bringing your uniform to school to change into before the game, you want to make sure you have absolutely everything you might need. These packing lists will help you get organized.

★ **GARMENT BAG:**
A garment bag, or hanging bag, can help you keep your uniform clean and wrinkle-free. Here's what can go inside:

SHELL (top or sweater)

SKIRT (or pants for a guy)

BODY LINER

WARM-UP

★ **YOUR CHEER BAG:**
If you don't have a garment bag, you can place your folded uniform in your cheer bag, along with the following essentials:

HAIR BOW

BRIEFS*

SPORTS BRA, or other appropriate undergarments

SOCKS*

CHEER SHOES

POMS

★ **SOME USEFUL EXTRAS YOU MAY WANT TO STASH IN YOUR CHEER BAG:**

WATER BOTTLE

HAIRBRUSH

EXTRA HAIR CLIPS, ELASTICS, BOBBY PINS

HAIR SPRAY

COSMETICS, including lip balm

SUNSCREEN FOR SUNNY FOOTBALL GAMES

HEALTHY SNACK (fruit, nuts, or a granola or protein bar)

GOOD LUCK CHARM

TEAM JACKET, WARM-UPS, OR SWEATS

SAFETY PINS (for last-minute wardrobe malfunctions)

TRAVEL PACK OF TISSUES AND/OR MAKEUP-REMOVER WIPES

STAIN-REMOVER STICK OR WIPES

* It's a good idea to allow an extra pair of cheer socks and briefs to "live" in your bag for emergencies. Even if you don't need them, a teammate might, and you can come to the rescue by lending her yours.

covering *the* costs

As with any extracurricular activity, cheerleading comes with some costs. Almost every squad has expenses that aren't covered by the school or sponsoring gym. You might be responsible for buying your cheer shoes, socks, briefs, and hair ribbons. Or you may have to pay for the whole uniform, poms, and megaphones, too. Camp fees will vary, depending on whether you attend an overnight camp at a fun resort or you have instructors come to your town. If you travel to faraway competitions, you might have the expenses of airline tickets and hotel rooms to consider.

All in all, the cost of cheerleading for a year can range between a few hundred and a few thousand dollars. But don't freak out if there's barely a jingle in your piggy bank! Your squad can do all kinds of fundraising to get the things you need—and have loads of fun at the same time!

Be a Sales Superstar

If you can sell the possibility of a come-from-behind victory to a crowd of nervous football fans, you can surely sell wrapping paper or soup mix in your community to make money for your squad.

Varsity.com offers some great fundraising opportunities for cheerleaders, such as selling spirit popcorn or lip balm.

When you're figuring out what to sell, think about the needs of your community and the timing of your efforts. Wrapping paper will be a winner if the holidays are approaching; lemonade mix might be a big hit if summer is right around the corner. Also consider how many people each cheerleader can reasonably sell to, and the profit potential of each order. Your squad could benefit a lot more if each customer buys a tote bag rather than a lollipop.

The company you're working with will use some of the money to pay for and provide the merchandise and to cover its own expenses; the rest (usually a prespecified percentage or a dollar amount per item) will be proceeds for your squad to use.

Spread Spirit Gear

Varsity.com also offers ways for you to combine fundraising with spirit-raising. You can get clothing, cups, mini-megaphones, or poms in school colors or with logos. Sell them at games, pep rallies, or other school events, and keep a portion of the proceeds for your squad.

Try to come up with a hilarious slogan for a T-shirt. If it becomes a must-have for every dedicated fan, your squad might get to travel first-class to competitions (or at least spring for a flight instead of a twelve-hour bus slog)!

Offer a Service

Providing a service can be even easier than selling products, because all you need are a few supplies; a time, date, and location; and a bunch of energetic cheerleaders (you already have those!). Services can be more lucrative, too, because the money you collect is 100 percent yours to keep.

Cheerleaders and car washes go together like round-offs and back handsprings. They're the perfect way to spend a hot, sunny day having fun with your friends and raising money for your squad. Get permission to use your school parking lot or another convenient, high-traffic location with a working water source. Spread the word to everyone you know who has a car, and post some signs for people in the community who might drive by. Stock up on sponges, soap, hoses, buckets, and old towels, and you're in business. People are always willing to shell out cash for a cheer-run car wash because they know it's for a good cause. And who doesn't like a sparkling-clean ride?

Or ask around to find out if anyone's parents or acquaintances need some help with their businesses. Cheerleaders from Paul Laurence Dunbar High School in Lexington, Kentucky, used to shine shoes during prom season at a local formal-wear shop owned by a fellow cheerleader's dad, with their wages going toward uniforms and competition costs.

Sweeten Someone's Day

Does your squad include any bakers? Do group sleepovers or squad get-togethers always include platters of homemade brownies or cookies? Consider a bake sale. Everyone can contribute a favorite treat to sell during lunch hour at school, at an extracurricular event, or somewhere else (in front of a grocery store, in your town square...just make sure to get permission in advance). For added fun, frost cupcakes in your team colors. Be sure to have nut-free and gluten-free options, which should be kept separate in clearly marked containers. It's nice to offer drinks, too, like bottled water or homemade lemonade.

You can also coordinate an exchange of flowers or holiday-themed treats, such as candy canes or chocolate hearts. Set up a table in the lunchroom and take orders. Customers can write a little note to the person they're buying for, seal it, then write the recipient's name on the outside. That night, get the squad together to attach the notes to the appropriate treats, and distribute them the following day. Candy and carnations are fairly inexpensive, and you may be able to negotiate a bulk discount from a local candy store or florist.

Get Creative

There are a million ways to raise money. Think about the special skills of your squad members, your connections through family and friends, and things that are going on in your community. Does the firehouse have bingo every Friday night? Maybe you can volunteer to sell raffle tickets for cash prizes and share the proceeds with the firefighters. Some college cheer squads create a calendar of photos that they sell on campus. Maybe your squad can get together to make beaded bracelets in school colors or customize holiday ornaments.

Just be sure you run all your ideas by a coach or school administrator before embarking on any of them; when money is involved, there are often legal and/or ethical concerns. And you might need someone to handle the big issues, like permits, permissions, and safety precautions. An adult can help you sort out what's feasible and practical and what isn't.

REAL CHEERLEADERS
REAL ANSWERS

What is your squad's go-to fundraiser? These cheerleaders found cool ways to raise money to cover their cheer costs.

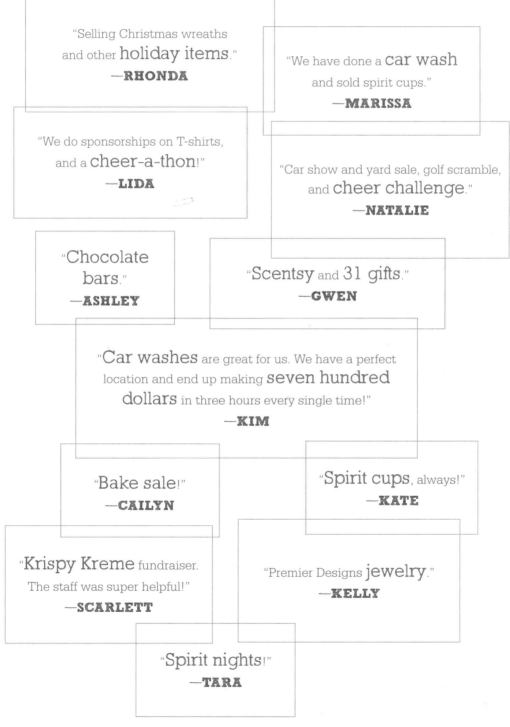

"Selling Christmas wreaths and other **holiday items**."
—**RHONDA**

"We have done a **car wash** and sold spirit cups."
—**MARISSA**

"We do sponsorships on T-shirts, and a **cheer-a-thon**!"
—**LIDA**

"Car show and yard sale, golf scramble, and **cheer challenge**."
—**NATALIE**

"Chocolate bars."
—**ASHLEY**

"**Scentsy** and 31 gifts."
—**GWEN**

"**Car washes** are great for us. We have a perfect location and end up making **seven hundred dollars** in three hours every single time!"
—**KIM**

"Bake sale!"
—**CAILYN**

"**Spirit cups**, always!"
—**KATE**

"**Krispy Kreme** fundraiser. The staff was super helpful!"
—**SCARLETT**

"Premier Designs **jewelry**."
—**KELLY**

"Spirit nights!"
—**TARA**

cheer-ity begins *at* home

A cheerleader's main focus is to support others—whether a specific sports team or a school community—and it's important to direct that "How can I help you?" attitude toward other people who live and work in your greater community.

Some schools and squads have specific community service requirements—anywhere from four to forty hours per year. But once you start volunteering, you might find the work so rewarding that you just don't want to stop. Some community service–oriented cheerleading squads rack up more than fifteen thousand hours of good works *every year.* "Our cheerleaders get out there and show the community what a valuable commodity they can be," says Kori Johnson, cheerleading coach of the Costa Mesa High School squads.

Want to get started but not sure where to begin? Just look around your hometown for ways that you and your squad can make an impact.

Get Involved with National School Spirit Day

Each year, cheering squads across the country combine spirit and service on National School Spirit Day. Go to nationalschoolspiritday.org for step-by-step instructions. On a predetermined day, usually in the fall, participating squads hold a pep rally to announce their community service project and invite classmates to join in. The project can be anything from cleaning up school grounds to raising funds for a specific charity.

You can have a lot of fun with this pep rally, maybe even creating new cheers and chants that incorporate the community service goal. Afterward, the cheerleaders and interested students get to work on the project. You can log your hours online and become eligible for great prizes at nationalschoolspiritday.org.

Approach Established Groups

Think about the organizations that are already doing great work in your community, such as soup kitchens, animal shelters, and services for the sick or disabled. Is there a children's advocacy organization or a senior citizens' center? Look out for walks or runs that raise money for cancer research or Alzheimer's disease. Some clubs raise money for scholarships for needy kids. And *all* these ventures need volunteers!

You could hand out water at a walkathon, wash dogs for a shelter, or waitress at a food festival that benefits the Make-A-Wish Foundation, like the Costa Mesa cheerleaders do. You might sell raffle tickets at a summer festival to support the local chamber of commerce. Or you could deliver Meals on Wheels.

Reach out to local organizations by phone or e-mail; your coach may want to do this, or you can designate a squad member, perhaps a captain, to organize your squad's community service work. Ask the organization how you can help out, and be ready to roll up your sleeves and do whatever is suggested. Or you can offer to perform in uniform* at one of the charity's events.

Organize a Food, Toy, or Clothing Drive

Your squad can gather food, toys, or clothing to donate to a local charity. Post signs around your school and have a few easily accessible designated drop-off areas, like boxes near the entrance of your gym. Make sure your signs explain the rules—for example, that toys must be brand-new and in their original boxes for safety reasons or that food should be canned or

---

* Always check with your coach to determine if this is permissible. There are often insurance concerns associated with this sort of event. It's most likely just a matter of getting the paperwork in order, and then you'll be good to go.

boxed nonperishable items. When it's time to deliver the donated goods, make sure you're all decked out in uniform to make the moment festive.

Every year, cheerleaders from Mascoutah High School in Illinois partner with their town's Moose Lodge for Operation Santa Claus. "We put boxes out at the school and at local businesses and get a list of families from our local township office," says coach Laurie Wager. "On the Saturday before Christmas, we organize the toys, divide the addresses, and go two or three girls to a car to deliver them. It's one of the most fun days of the year. Afterward we go caroling to local businesses and then go for pizza."

Another time, the squad heard about a cheerleading team in inner-city Chicago that didn't have the funds to buy cheer shoes. "We decided to bring in all the extra shoes we had that were still in great condition," says Laurie. The squad also contacted other area schools that had the same colors—blue and white—and mascot as the school in Chicago. They donated

poms and spirit gear, sending so much stuff that some of it was passed on to a nearby school. "The coach sent a picture of the squad in all their new gear. They looked so excited! It was a great experience," says Laurie.

Visit a Children's Hospital or Nursing Home

Schedule a visit through the hospital or nursing home administrators and then show up in full cheerleading regalia. You can chat with children who are being treated for illnesses or injuries and elderly people who don't make it to too many football games anymore. You might even show off a few cheers and simple stunts. It's always nice to leave each person with a little memento of your visit—such as a colorful minipom, or something seasonal, like flowers in May or candy canes around the holidays. "Penn State Mont Alto cheerleaders visit Hershey Medical Center to 'cheer' up the children there who are battling cancer. Always a memorable and fulfilling community service project for our team," says Christina Yoder.

Figure out how else you can help bring smiles to people's faces. Cheerleaders from Blackman High School in Murfreesboro, Tennessee, assist at a "prom" held for local senior citizens. The cheerleaders dress up in formal wear and dance with the elders. They also help out at an Easter egg hunt for local kids.

Adopt a Park, Highway, or Waterway

Set aside a Saturday morning or Sunday afternoon and head down to a public area that could use a bit of a spruce-up. (Run this idea by your local parks department first, and get some suggestions on the areas that really need help.) Bring trash bags, or even rakes, shovels, and some no-fuss flowers, and beautify the outdoor spaces where kids play and adults enjoy their leisure time. "We picked up trash along the back roads where I live," says Charleigh Renee, of Erlanger, Kentucky.

Always Be Ready

It happens. Homes burn down and hurricanes blow through town, so be prepared to spring into action whenever there's a need. Contact a family that has lost their home to a disaster and help them clean up their property and salvage their belongings. And keep an ear out for quieter needs. The Blackman High School cheerleaders heard that a classmate in a wheelchair needed a specially designed home, so they joined forces with Habitat for Humanity and built him one!

Take Five

When you hear about an illness, accident, or other tragedy affecting someone in your community—or even far away—have each squad member write and send a supportive card (or one person can collect them and send them as a batch). "It takes five minutes to do, but the impact it can have on a person's life is amazing," says Laurie Wager, the coach of the Mascoutah High School cheerleaders. "That's what I'm trying to teach, that it doesn't have to be monumental. It can be something very small and have a huge impact."

Once your cheering squad develops a reputation for community service, you won't have to work too hard to come up with ideas for projects. People and organizations will be coming to *you,* and your only regret will be that you don't have more time to help them.

"People ask the cheerleaders, what does this do for you? I heard one kid say it's not about what it does for me, it's about what it does for someone else," says Laurie. Still, you'll love the warm feeling you get from helping out people in need, and you'll develop more intense bonds with the squad members beside you as you're cleaning up a riverbank or making sandwiches for a soup kitchen.

"It eliminates some of the drama and puts things in perspective," says Laurie. "You think, maybe my issues aren't so big, when you're out there doing something for someone who has a lot less than you."

And community service will serve you for the rest of your life, even after (sniff!) your cheering career is finished. "One of my cheerleaders went on to join the army, and she won the community service award there. She did *every* project that came up because it was second nature to her," says Kori Johnson, coach of Costa Mesa High School. "Community service work shapes who you're going to be in the future. Besides making good cheerleaders, we're also making good people."

REAL CHEERLEADERS REAL ANSWERS

What is the best part about being a cheerleader?
We got a lot of amazing responses to this question!
Sounds like there are *many* great things about being
a cheerleader...but we knew that already!

"EVERYTHING! Building a great big family with the team, learning new routines and tricks! The competitions are fun, too! You get all nervous but you have your cheer family there with you. Then once you all hit the blue mat it's like, BOOM! Instant freedom! Everything about cheerleading is the best, even falling and getting those aches and bruises, because it only shows people how strong cheerleaders are."
—CHASE

"Being seen as a role model and inspiring others."
—LEXII

"That moment when your music starts, you bring on the fierceness and show those judges who owns the mat. Being there with your whole team, working together and hitting everything flawlessly. The pounding of the beat in your ears. The passion to hit every motion perfectly, and when the routine is over, you are out of breath and tired but it was worth it. Every single second of it."
—MARGARET

"The opportunity to do amazing things, inspire people, put smiles on the faces in the crowd!"
—CRISELDA

"Cheerleading has shown me how important it is to have faith in something, and how contagious and unifying positive energy can be. It's amazing to see other people excited about the same thing I'm excited for, and it feels even better to know that I helped foster that energy for them."
—BETANIA

"Hearing the **crowd roar** once you've hit your pass that you've worked all year to get. I will always **love tumbling**. Even if it's just a quick back tuck for a friend, it's my **favorite feeling** in the world."

—HALYN

"The best part about being a cheerleader is the **experience** and the **life lessons**. We learn so much about how to be a better person and bring spirit into other people's lives."

—DANIELLE

"Being able to encourage people to be the **best** at anything they do and let them know that they can do that!"

—MORGANNE

"All the **friends** you make, whether it's on your own team, other students, or cheerleaders from other schools."

—MELISSA

"The best thing is the **sense of family** between everyone and knowing that you **always have your team** to back you up. If I am down I can always depend on them for anything. I love being able to talk to them no matter what, and even if there are some problems we always come back together on the mat."

—EMILY

"I love being a cheerleader because it makes me so **happy**. It is **my life**, and I wouldn't be the person I am without it."

—PAIGE

"Getting to spend every day with my teammates (**I call them sisters**!) and just doing something I love."

—ALEX

CAPTAIN'S CORNER

Most cheering squads have at least one captain or team leader. These are members of the squad who help make decisions for the team, such as which cheers you'll do when, how practices are run, and what uniform you'll wear. Captains might also take the lead in organizing carpools and community service work. If you're named to this role, whether by coach's decree or by the vote of all squad members, you have a lot of (rewarding!) work ahead of you. Here's how to do it best:

LEAD BY EXAMPLE

"If you're going to ask someone to do something, make sure you're doing it yourself first," advises Ryan Martin, a former cheerleading captain at Paul Laurence Dunbar High School in Kentucky as well as the University of Alabama. Demonstrate, through your own hair and makeup and uniform, how you want your squad to look. If you want them to be on time, you'd better be on time. And if you need people to roll out the mats before practice, get out there and show them how it's done.

STAY ORGANIZED

"I use a mass text message to keep everyone on schedule and tell them what to wear to games," says Allie Farrell, a two-time captain of the cheerleading squad of Western Kentucky University. You might also be the person responsible for creating the packing list for away games, or bringing the signs or poms to the pep rally. If you forget anything, you'll let the whole team down.

KNOW THE GAME

You need to know more than the rules of cheerleading—you also need to understand basketball or football or whichever sport you're supporting. As captain, you decide which cheers to perform when, so you don't want to start "HOLD THAT LINE, IT'S THIRD DOWN!" when it should be "FIRST AND TEN, DO IT AGAIN!" Always pay attention to what's going on in the game, as well as what's happening with your squad on the sidelines.

HANDLE DISAGREEMENTS

It's inevitable. The top girl wants to do a full down, while her bases want to stick with an extension straight cradle. One cheerleader wants the squad to show off a new routine, while another says she's not ready. As a captain, you should step in and help resolve such problems. But if things are too out of hand, bring in the coach. "You can let the coach be the bad guy, because the cheerleaders can be mad at the coach if they want, but you have to work with them," says Ryan.

DON'T PLAY FAVORITES

Of course, you might be BFFs with some of the people on your squad, while others roll with a different crew, but as a captain, you need to treat everyone well. Listen to what each person has to say and find a way to treat them fairly. This *doesn't* mean you must treat everyone exactly the same. Different things motivate different people. "You can be tough with some people and they really respond well to that, while you have to give others lots of positive feedback," says Ryan.

COMMUNICATE WITH THE COACH

As captain, you're the one who needs to call the coach at eleven o'clock the night before the game to tell her that one of your top girls has the flu. And you're the one who'll field your coach's requests—for example, time to switch to football sweaters—and relay them to the rest of the squad. "Have respect for your coach," says Allie. "And don't try to *be* another coach. Don't step too far in, where the other cheerleaders think of you just as a boss and not someone they can also be friends with."

part

3

CHEER NATION: INSPIRING CHEERLEADERS AND SQUADS

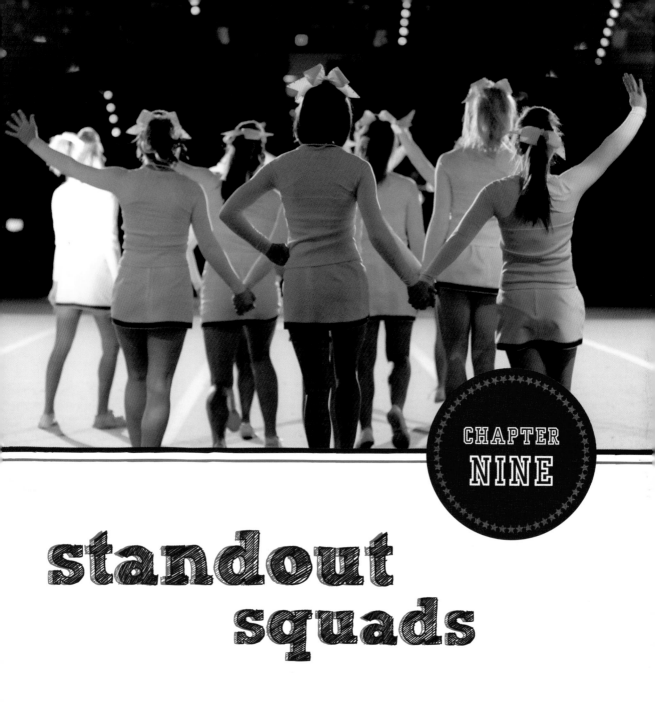

standout squads

If you pay close attention to cheerleading competitions—the ones that take place in your hometown, or the ones broadcast nationally on TV—you'll probably start to notice something pretty amazing. Squads from the same schools tend to take home the top trophies year after year after year. The varsity all-girl squad from Greenup County High School in Greenup, Kentucky, has won the UCA National High School Cheerleading Championship fourteen times since 1981. The coed team from Sparkman High School in Harvest, Alabama, has won eleven titles since 1993. And repeat winners happen on the college level, too.

These schools have winning traditions and infuse their communities with pride and cheerleading spirit. "We want the little girls in the stands counting down the days until they can wear the red and white and cheer for the Bearcats, just like we did when we were that age," says Heather Reeder, coach of the Ruston High School cheerleaders in Ruston, Louisiana, whose squads have won numerous NCA titles. Once they grow up and join the squad, they're ready to make all the sacrifices and do all the hard work necessary to become the best.

If your squad hasn't burst onto the national scene yet, don't let this news about other schools' decades of winnings discourage you. There's always room for newcomers, and every powerhouse squad once stood on the podium for the very first time. And if your squad prefers to spend all its energy supporting the school and sports teams, that's noble, too. But if you do have the itch to compete at the highest levels, you can get some good advice from those who've gone there before.

EXPECTATIONS OF GREATNESS

Cheerleaders who become champions know where they're headed even before they make the squad. Those trying out for the Morehead State University cheering teams, for example, are well aware that the school has previously taken home more than thirty national titles. "The big thing at Morehead is to do it for the people who came before you," explains Ronnie Patrick, a member of the squad that won in 2012 and 2013. "It motivated us. We didn't want to be the team that didn't win."

These hopes can drive cheerleaders' training—you might take the extra tumbling class or spend a few extra hours each week lifting weights at the gym so that you'll be able to send a top girl even higher in a basket toss—because you know that one day, a national championship could depend on it.

And once you're named to the squad, the intention to win a championship will infuse all your efforts to come together as a team and reach your potential. "It begins at the very first practice," says Caity Hinshaw, a member of Indiana University's 2012 and 2013 national championship all-girl squad. "The leaders say, 'This is what we expect of you,' and you take on that mentality from the very beginning."

"Our girls are told from day one, the team that works the hardest is the team that wins the most," says Donna Martin, cheerleading coach for Paul Laurence Dunbar High School in Lexington, Kentucky, whose squads have won eight national championships since 1995. "'Together We Win' has been a longtime expression for our program."

You can set the tone and expect greatness from yourself and your squad—and you'll be much more likely to achieve it!

PRACTICE MAKES PERFECT

Don't make any major plans for the holidays! At least, not if you're hoping to make a name for yourself at a major cheerleading competition. With many national competitions taking place in January or February, the top squads spend much of December in the gym—even as some of their classmates are going on ski trips or celebrating the New Year on a Caribbean cruise.

"From September on, we practice as we are going to compete," says Dan Harrod, coach of Bob Jones High School in Madison, Alabama, which has won five national championships over the past eight years. "Repetition for us is the key to success, so when the girls hit the floor, they are always confident in their skills. It's the preparation before that will make you successful at the end."

At every practice, hold yourself to the highest standard by giving every jump, chant, and stunt your all, and encourage your squadmates to do the same. "Teammates need to hold each other responsible for their work ethic and dedication," says Dunbar's Donna Martin. "A cheer squad is the ultimate example of a team working together because you cannot just rotate players in a game. All pieces of the puzzle must be present and fit together."

Keep your goals in mind at every practice. Los Alamitos (California) High School cheerleaders use discipline and hard work to master their routines, "hoping to one day [wear] the jacket of a champion," explains their coach, Cheryl Vuong.

BRINGING IT TO THE COMPETITION

Every year, just before Greenup County High School's cheerleaders head to Nationals, they invite friends and family to watch them perform their routine full out. "That's when we realize the tradition we have supporting us, and to live up to," says coach Candy Berry. The squads then head to Orlando, Florida, ready to present their A game.

"Take pride in your school and remember that you leave a legacy behind," says coach Heather Reeder of Ruston High School. "What do you want that legacy to be?"

Each squad has its own competition-day traditions and superstitions. Some sit in the stands and cheer for all the other competitors; others avert their eyes and try to distract one another from feeling nervous. "We don't watch any other teams; we focus on what we have to do to perform our routine to the best of our ability," says Lisa Holladay Aderholt, coach of the Sparkman High School cheerleaders. "After warm-ups, the kids pray together and do silly handshakes before being introduced. After they compete, they talk about their performance—the good and bad points and how it could have been improved."

For their big moment on the mat, some squads remove any troublesome elements from their routines and replace them with another stunt or tumbling pass they are sure to hit. "We like to put the best solid routine on the floor," says Bob Jones High School's Dan Harrod. "Some years other teams might have more skill, but after those two and a half minutes, a team that hits solid stands closer to the top than the bottom."

Other competitors use their adrenaline to put up their most intricate stunts and throw their most difficult tumbling passes, and hope that their nerves don't make them unsteady. "Our squad is known for performing cutting-edge routines and maxing out the difficulty," says Jomo K. Thompson, coach of the University of Kentucky, which has won nineteen titles. The tactic that leads to the top trophy all depends on the day and the performance.

Every great squad showcases its strengths—and quirks. "We stress technique and always making a stunt look easy," says Jon Summerville, coach of Graves County High School, a six-time championship squad from Mayfield, Kentucky.

"We were the first to introduce advanced tumbling into cheerleading. We amazed people with our precise execution of group tumbling in the early 1980s," says Candy Berry from Greenup County High School. "And people tease us about our socks! We don't know if they like them or not, but it's our trademark." In an era of no-see-um socks that hide inside cheer shoes, Greenup's bunchy white socks go all the way up to the cheerleaders' calves.

Socks, stunts, and spirit to spare—every squad tries to be at their best on competition day.

HOORAY for HOLLYWOOD

Cheerleaders often appear on TV and in the movies—remember Sandy in *Grease*?—but in recent years, they've gotten some serious screen time. *Bring It On*, released in 2000, became a cult classic and spawned sequels and a Broadway musical! And the TV series *Glee* highlighted all sorts of cheerleader issues through the characters of Quinn, Brittany, Santana, Becky, and of course the tough-on-the-outside, sweet-on-the-inside coach Sue Sylvester.

Many of the Hollywood portrayals are positive—showing cheerleaders working hard, being kind, and having a lot of fun. Sometimes, though, inaccurate stereotypes are suggested—for example, that cheerleaders are ditzy or mean.

Everyone involved in the cheer world knows this is off base. Cheerleaders are usually among the friendliest, most outgoing, and most academically driven students at school. So don't buy into the negatives coming out of Tinseltown, and instead make it part of your mission to prove the truth: that cheerleaders are good people devoted to improving themselves, their squads, their schools, and the world around them.

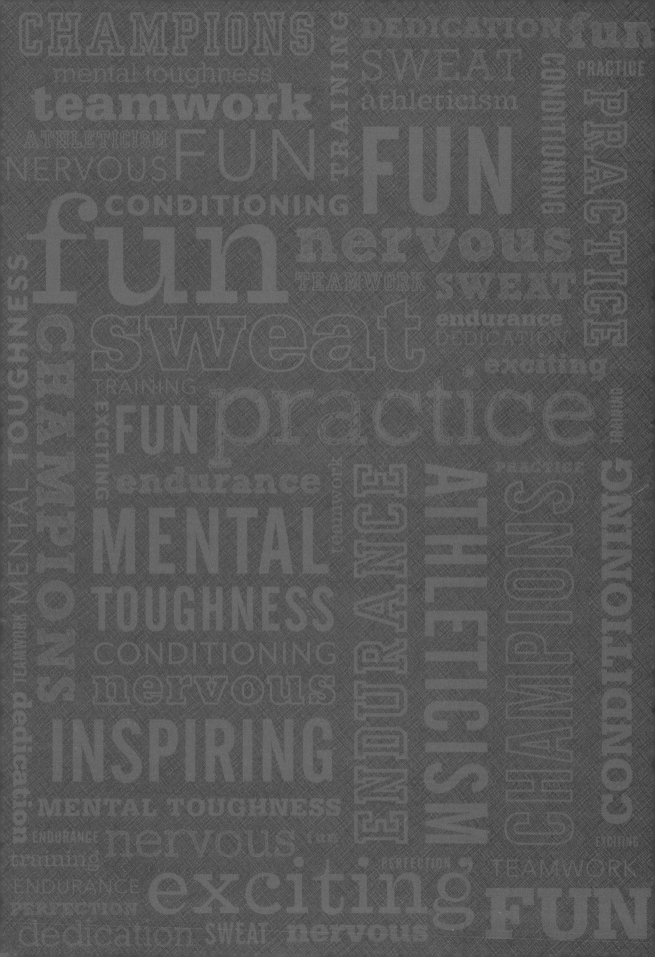

leading
the way

Cheerleading can be challenging. It's not easy to master the skills and then perform them perfectly in front of the packed bleachers at a football game or the judges at Nationals! Now imagine trying to do so with a disability, after a life-threatening illness, or while your town is recovering from a horrible natural disaster. The cheerleaders and squads you'll meet in this chapter have done exactly that. They've managed to excel as cheerleaders in spite of, or perhaps *because* of, some tremendous obstacles tossed into their life path. With extraordinary determination and tenacity, these cheerleaders give new meaning to the word *victory*. We think they're simply amazing. And faced with a similar set of hard circumstances, we know that you would be, too.

Finding a Way

PATIENCE BEARD

As a tiny baby, Patience Beard had her leg amputated as a result of a birth defect that left her with a too-short femur (thighbone). But having a prosthetic leg has never slowed her down. "I've had it my whole life, so I don't know what it would be like to not have it," she says.

While she was growing up in Texarkana, Texas, her parents encouraged her to try every activity that interested her. "If it didn't work the first time, they helped me find a way around it," she says. For example: she struggled to ride a bike because it was hard to keep her prosthetic foot on the pedal. "My dad and I talked about it, and he cut a strap off his golf bag and attached it to the pedal, to keep my foot in," she says. "There's always a way to do things when you really set your mind to it."

Next, Patience set her mind on gymnastics. "It was challenging for me, but it's hard for everyone to learn to throw your body in the air," she says. "I wasn't competitive, but I loved tumbling." She took her skills to all star cheer, then joined her middle school and high school cheerleading squads. When she enrolled at the University of Arkansas, she decided to go out for the squad there, too. "I love football and the SEC atmosphere," she says. "I knew I was going to cheer for the team anyway, so why not do it on the field?"

Competition at tryouts was fierce, and only four freshman girls made the squad. Patience was among them. "Switching from all-girl to coed stunting was hard," she says. "I had to go from trusting three people to keep you up and catch you on the way down, to just one guy who I just met. It's a lot more challenging, but that's why I love it so much more."

She rocks her zebra-striped prosthetic leg with her cardinal-red Razorbacks uniform during the school year, and joined the staff of UCA in the summer to teach camps across the country. She's a mentor and an inspiration to children at the hospital where she gets her checkups, and to the kids she meets at camps.

"Every person has their own obstacles," she says. "It's really about finding the best way for yourself. You're only limited to what you tell yourself you're limited to."

Cheering Past Autism

ALEXIS WINEMAN

Alexis Wineman glided onto the stage during the 2013 Miss America pageant and confidently took the microphone to perform a comedic skit. No one would have ever guessed that the gorgeous Miss Montana was autistic. And that cheerleading had helped her overcome it.

"I was scared of social interaction as a child; I just didn't know what to say in front of people," she explains. Her parents noticed her troubles and sought out specialists who could help, but they also realized Alexis could function reasonably well, so they pushed her to confront her challenges.

"My mom was the cheerleading coach, and she forced me to join the squad as a high school freshman to get me to interact with people I didn't know," explains Alexis. At first, she struggled with dealing with the other girls. And she had to conquer her fear of stunting. As the smallest girl on the squad, "they wanted to make me a top, but I was so scared."

Alexis quit cheering her sophomore year at Cut Bank High School, but to her surprise she found she really missed it, and returned to the squad as a junior. Then things started falling into place. "I did become a top, and I could also base and back-spot. I felt super useful; it was a great feeling!" she says. She also got along easily with the other girls on the squad, and was named captain for her senior year.

That's when she really hit her stride. She and another girl on the squad were invited to New York to perform in the Macy's Thanksgiving Day Parade. "I was bouncing off the walls when we got the letter," she says. "Being a girl from a small town in Montana, you don't think these opportunities are open for you." They traveled to New York for the event. "The strange thing was, I wasn't scared! I felt if I'd been thrown into that situation without cheer, I would have been freaking out."

Emboldened, she decided to participate in the Miss Montana pageant as a way to possibly earn scholarship money for college, and walked away with the crown. In 2013, she was the youngest contestant to take the stage at the Miss America pageant, and the first ever with an autism diagnosis.

"I still have good days and bad," she says. "Little things that neurotypical people can do, like make eye contact, or talk to strangers, or tolerate the sound of air-conditioning, can seem like an Olympic sport to me." She credits cheerleading and participating in Miss Montana with helping her function better in the world and giving her opportunities that many girls only dream of.

Scholarship in hand, she's now heading off to Huntingdon College in Alabama, where she'll study communications and art and continue to show the world what autistic people can do.

Doing What She Loves

ERICA OUFNAC

Erica Oufnac has been lighting up the sidelines since she was eight, when she joined a cheerleading squad that supported a community football team. In high school, she competed at Nationals as a member of the Live Oak High School squad. But as a freshman in college, she decided to take a hiatus, walking away from her spot on Louisiana State University's alternate squad in order to work as a cheering coach at a local gym while focusing on school.

A few months later, she started having some strange physical symptoms. "I was having trouble breathing whenever I lay down," Erica says. "I thought it was just allergies, but then I woke up one morning and my left arm was swollen." When the swelling didn't go down, she visited her doctor, who was worried that she had some sort of blockage. Further testing detected a tumor in her chest, and Erica was diagnosed with non-Hodgkin's lymphoma.

Surgery to remove the tumor would be too risky, so Erica headed to St. Jude Children's Research Hospital in Memphis, Tennessee, for chemotherapy treatments. Doctors hoped the treatments would eliminate the tumor, though chemotherapy also made her feel very sick. "I had days when I didn't want to get out of bed, and there were times I left the contents of my stomach in the nearest parking lot," recalls Erica. "For four months, my whole life was just treatment."

St. Jude covered all her costs—as it does for all its patients—even housing her nearby and paying for travel to and from her home. "Every day we got a thirty-dollar meal card to eat in the cafeteria, or a hundred-dollar gift card for groceries when we were staying in the housing," she explains. "They have movies, a playground, a game room, workout facilities, even a hair salon"—though she didn't need that last one. "I lost my hair in late August," she says.

Happily for Erica, the treatments worked and the disease went into remission. The first year afterward is the riskiest for relapse, but Erica made it through safely and is well on her way to the five-year mark, when her doctors will consider her cured. "I was never worried about dying," she says. "I knew I was in good hands at St. Jude and they were going to save me."

But the experience did make her rethink how she was living her life. "Once I'd recovered, I thought to myself: *I'm young and healthy now. I need to be doing what I love.* So I decided to get back to cheer."

Having transferred to Southeastern Louisiana University, Erica attended an open practice for the cheerleading squad at the urging of a friend. She impressed the coach, who suggested she finish out the season with the squad. "There I was on the sidelines with my little buzz cut, and it was great!" Erica says. That May, she tried out again and made the squad, and the following year she joined the UCA instructional staff, traveling across the country to teach at cheering camps. "This is something I can do and want to do," she says. "I'm more motivated now since having the cancer. It wasn't a bad thing, in my opinion."

A Tornado Destroyed Their School but Not Their Spirit

JOPLIN HIGH SCHOOL

When May 22, 2011, dawned in Joplin, Missouri, the varsity cheerleaders from Joplin High School were planning a summer of fun, as well as practices for competitions and the fast-approaching football season. Then, at 5:41 PM, a vicious tornado tore through the town.

"It was high school graduation day and we had about ten minutes to take cover," says Kristen Hermann, coach of the Joplin High School cheerleaders. In the eerie aftermath, "no one could get ahold of anyone because the cell phone towers went down; there was so much traffic because there were power lines in the street. It was awful."

The tornado destroyed eight thousand homes and businesses and took 161 lives. Joplin High School was demolished, and six of the sixteen cheerleaders lost their homes. "My house was hit in the tornado, so we had to move. And my high school got hit," says Emma Cox, captain of the varsity squad. "So my whole life changed."

Four days after the tornado, the cheerleaders met with their coach. How could they go on in the wake of such devastation? "We decided we were going to continue with competition," says Kristen. "So the next day, we went and learned our routine. I think some people were a little hesitant at first, but when all was said and done, I really feel it made us closer."

Meanwhile, school authorities were scrambling to create new high school facilities. They converted a vacant building near the mall into a school. It wasn't easy to start over in a new place. "There were so many memories in that high school, and traditions we were wanting to have our senior year. It's never going to be the same," says Emma. But the cheerleaders decided to make the best of the situation, and by October they were promoting the "Lost at Sea" homecoming theme with fun decorations, a wild spirit week, and a pep rally. At the homecoming football game, the squad cheered, chanted, danced, and engaged the fans. "We just pump up the crowd and make sure everybody's having a great time," says cheerleader Michelle Turner.

Picking up the pieces immediately after the disaster and pushing forward toward their goals turned out to be the right decision. "I think it really helped give the girls a sense of normalcy," explains Coach Hermann, "and let them know we could still survive this and that we could pull together through everything."

Rather than shifting the squad off their axis, the tornado gave the Joplin High School cheerleaders some extra go-get-'em. "I feel like they have a lot more energy because they have seen the overwhelming support that we have gotten not only from our community, but from people that we don't even know across the world. It has just been so unbelievable. And we all truly feel so blessed," says Kristen.

community
service stars

Cheerleaders across the country are constantly going into their communities to serve the needy. Their kindness and optimism have spawned so many smiles. They've raised countless dollars for good causes. And their efforts have improved many individuals' lives. The work of some cheerleaders and squads can even have a national or global impact. These community service stars' ideas have spread to schools all over the country, and their outstanding execution has earned them headlines, honors, and awards. Check out their stories and get inspired to do good! These are examples of why America needs cheerleaders!

Cheer for All

SARAH CRONK

"If we all work together, we can change game night in America forever." —Sarah Cronk

In 2008, four members of the cheering squad from Pleasant Valley High School in Bettendorf, Iowa, volunteered at the Iowa Special Olympics, where people with disabilities competed in athletic events. The cheerleaders performed at the opening ceremony and helped with a clinic that taught cheering to the athletes.

While they were there, a lightbulb went on for the squad members, including Sarah Cronk. "It became abundantly clear how easy it was to adapt cheerleading to different skill levels," she says. "The athletes could really shine at it."

Sarah had already been thinking about how students with disabilities could get more involved in school activities. Her own brother, Charlie, is on the autism spectrum, and she had witnessed his painful transition to high school, which eased only after an older boy convinced him to join the swim team. "It gave him a sense of belonging and really changed his world," says Sarah. "It clicked with me that this could really work within cheerleading."

She consulted her coach and then her principal, and both green-lighted the idea. With the help of some of her squadmates, she reached out to local organizations, e-mailed the school board LIST-SERV, and posted flyers around town. Soon, five kids with disabilities had signed up, and they were matched with five cheerleaders called "peer coaches." The new team was named the Sparkles. "We wanted a name that was cute and fun and that went with our mascot, the Spartans," Sarah explains.

The cheerleaders would hold their regular practice, then take a fifteen-minute break and join up with the Sparkles, who learned cheers, chants, jumps, and stunts. The teams performed right alongside each other on the sidelines of football games. "Everyone loved it," says Sarah. "People started referring to what the Sparkles had done for our community as the Sparkle Effect. They broke down social barriers between students with and without disabilities, because now they had something in common to talk about."

The program's popularity had one downside, though. Soon, there were more Sparkle hopefuls than her squad could include. "It never felt right to me to turn people away," says Sarah.

So she launched the Sparkle Effect, an organization that helps other schools and communities implement the program, by offering a quick-start kit. It's been adopted by more than one hundred squads—many cheerleaders and some dance teams, too—in at least thirty-five states. Sarah still runs the organization.

"The Sparkle Effect has broken down perceptions of what people with disabilities can do," she says. "The Spartan Sparkles are more spirited than anyone I've ever seen in my life!"

Reading for All

HANNAH McRAE YOUNG

> "I either had my nose in a book or was at the gym tumbling." —*Hannah McRae Young*

Hannah McRae Young, of Kernersville, North Carolina, was a freshman at East Forsyth High School with a state-mandated community service requirement to meet and a crazy-busy schedule packed with all star cheerleading, high school cheerleading, and a ton of tough classes. "I needed to make up my own project, so I took the two things I loved the most and stuck them together," she says. "CheeReaders was born."

The daughter of an English teacher and children's book reviewer, Hannah McRae had been surrounded by books from a very early age: "I loved *Goodnight Moon* and the whole Harry Potter series," she says. She even coauthored some children's book reviews with her mother for the local newspaper, the *Winston-Salem Journal*.

She wanted to spread her love of reading to children who didn't have access to many books or who didn't get much one-on-one attention at home. She contacted a local kindergarten for permission to come in and read with the children. The little ones were super impressed by her cheering background—one time they made her perform a cheer in the classroom, so she improvised and changed the words from "PICK IT UP!" to "READ IT UP!"—and they soon echoed her enthusiasm for books, too.

Hannah McRae recruited some of her fellow cheerleaders to join her—and the idea started spreading through her town. "Kids at the other high school in town heard about it and decided they wanted to read, too. They went to other elementary schools, and it grew from there," she explains.

As more and more cheerleaders expressed interest in being a CheeReader—they also wanted to encourage small children to spend more time with books and improve their literacy skills—Hannah McRae developed a website to help people implement the volunteer program for their own squads. Squads from almost every state have asked for information about CheeReaders, and it has been implemented in Canada, too! Through much experimentation, Hannah McRae learned that the program works best with children from kindergarten through second grade, and that it's better to read to the kids one-on-one.

"The kids get so excited when their very own cheerleader comes to read with them," says Hannah McRae. While most are a bit shy at first, they warm up fast when they get to shake poms or get into a great story. One little girl would run to Hannah McRae as soon as she entered the classroom, hug her leg, and not let go until they settled down with a book.

When Hannah McRae went off to college at Auburn University, she handed the reins of the program to Varsity so that she could focus on her education (though she remains on the board of directors). She's now active in her sorority and working on a way to bring CheeReaders to college, because she misses sharing her lifelong love of reading with children who are just starting to sound out words.

"It's amazing to see where the children start off and where they end up at the end of a year with CheeReaders," says Hannah McRae.

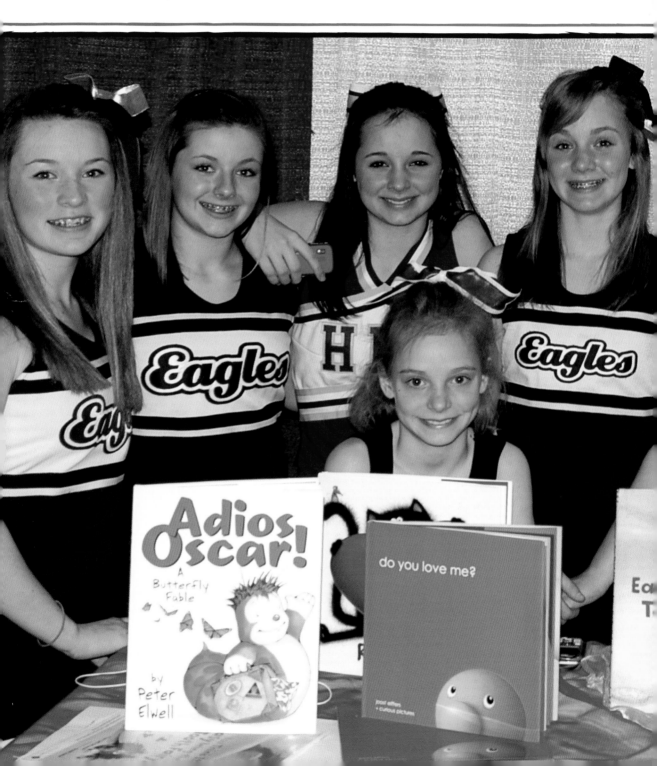

REAL CHEERLEADERS
REAL ANSWERS

What is the most common misconception about cheerleaders?

They're ruthless, vain, and buy hair spray by the case? Umm...no! Cheerleaders set the record straight.

"That it doesn't take much work. It is *very* **hard work** and for whoever doesn't think so, come watch a practice. You'll be tired from just watching."
—**ANTHONY**

"That we have bleached blond hair, fake nails, and tons of makeup."
—**JULIE**

"That we think that we are better than everyone else. We know that **we are normal people**, too."
—**STARR**

"Just because we dance and smile does not mean we do not work as hard as a basketball player. I also find it very frustrating when people say the word *cheerleader* as a stereotype for a person who is not academic. Cheerleaders can be **independent women** and very **brainy**!"
—**VIKKI**

"People think cheerleaders don't really do anything but wear short skirts at school. They think we spend our entire practice doing cheers without understanding the extent of cheerleading—the **stunting**, the **skills** it takes, the **conditioning** we have to do."
—**BRIANNA**

"I think the biggest misconception about cheerleaders is that we are all stupid and mean. My team is made up of the **sweetest** and **smartest** girls I know. I think people really need to get to know us before they judge us."
—**ALYSSA**

"The biggest misconception about cheerleaders is that we are all dumb blondes. On my squad we are a mix of backgrounds, personalities, and appearances. We all strive for **academic excellence**, and most of us make **honor roll**!"
—**GABY**

"That we are all snobs and we are the most popular people. When in fact we are normal people with the same amount of homework and the same problems as everyone else. We're just **trying to fit in**."
—**MELISSA**

True Holiday Spirit

ARCHBISHOP CARROLL HIGH SCHOOL, WASHINGTON, DC

"I knew I could count on the cheerleaders."
—Teacher Megan O'Hara

Archbishop Carroll High School in Washington, DC, has a long tradition of community service. "It's part of the mission of the school," says Megan O'Hara, who taught the school's social justice class and coordinated students' service efforts. The school's cheerleaders play a leading role in many of the service endeavors.

For more than fifty years, the school has conducted a massive food drive every November. In 2012 alone, the students collected 45,000 pounds of food. "Some say it's the biggest school food drive in the country," says Megan. The students canvass neighborhoods during the week, dropping off paper bags with flyers telling residents what they can donate and when someone will come back to pick up the bags. On weekends, the students return to the neighborhoods in buses to collect the offerings. They bring them back to the school and weigh, sort, and distribute them into boxes that are given out to hundreds of families in need. "Each family gets two large boxes of food plus a turkey," says Megan. Just in time for a bountiful Thanksgiving dinner!

Cheerleading coach Tina Colbert drives one of the collection buses every Sunday, and fills it with cheerleaders (her daughter among them). "If I needed people to be there, I knew I could count on the cheerleaders," says Megan. And some years, the cheerleaders up the ante by challenging the football team or basketball team to see which group can bring in the most food.

In recent years, the male athletes haven't stood a chance against the cheerleading squad, which harbors a secret weapon: Abigail Bradley. She single-handedly collected over one thousand pounds of food—more than any other student in the school! Abigail's dream is to one day open a food pantry to help people in need. "She has said she wants to give her life to something meaningful, and she finds a lot of meaning in helping the hungry," says Megan.

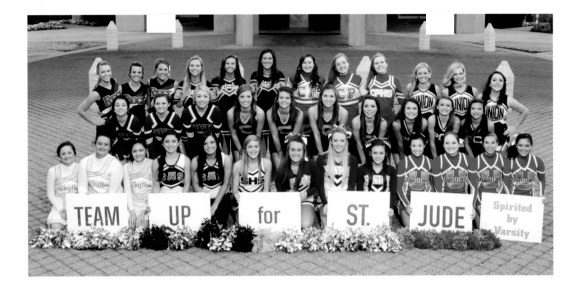

Team Up for St. Jude

PRESBYTERIAN CHRISTIAN SCHOOL, HATTIESBURG, MISSISSIPPI

"We were totally amazed."
—Cheerleading coach Donna Bielstein

The cheerleaders from Presbyterian Christian School in Hattiesburg, Mississippi, understood all too well the enormously important work of St. Jude Children's Research Hospital, which helps children with cancer and other catastrophic diseases. A schoolmate had been treated there as a young child but ultimately died of her disease in the eighth grade. "I don't think I can talk about her without crying," says Donna Bielstein, the JV cheerleading coach and a teacher at the school. So when the JV squad had the chance to raise money to help other suffering children, through Varsity's "Team Up for St. Jude," they gave it their all. At cheer camp, Varsity asked participating girls to turn in five to ten fundraising letters addressed to personal contacts—grandparents, aunts and uncles, family friends, neighbors. Varsity then tracked how much each cheerleader and each team raised, with all the proceeds going directly to St. Jude. "Instead of five to ten, I made my girls do fifteen to twenty letters," explains Donna. "They said, 'Why?' I said, 'We never ask why. In everything we do, we go above and beyond.'" One cheerleader used her family's holiday card list and printed out the address labels. "She turned in a hundred!" says Donna.

Still, it was a happy surprise when the squad learned they were among the top ten fundraising teams and earned an invitation for three squad representatives and their coach to visit St. Jude. Donna chose the girls whose efforts had paid off the most, and they made the five-hour drive to Memphis.

"We just walked around with our mouths open because we were totally amazed," says Donna. "The fact that it doesn't smell like a hospital, that they have a four-star chef on duty. We did karaoke with the patients and had a barbecue. It was an awesome trip."

The girls returned home psyched to take on the fundraising challenge again and to vie for the top spots on the squad. "One of the little girls who went said, 'You're not getting my place,'" says Donna.

St. Jude costs about 1.8 million dollars *per day* to run. And incredibly, families whose children are treated there don't pay the hospital a cent. In addition, all the research done at the hospital is made available to anyone who needs it, absolutely free. "They don't care about credit," explains Donna. "They just want to cure cancer for these kids."

When the Presbyterian cheerleaders marveled at the huge costs the hospital absorbed, Donna told them, "It's the letters you sent out, the pennies you raised—that's how they do it."

Does your squad have any special traditions or customs?

"We all **sign each other's shoes** at the end of the year."
—**KAITLYN**

"My squad has the '**positive box.**' Whenever someone on our team does something awesome or gets a new skill, we write little anonymous notes and put them in the positive box. We read them to the entire team during **team bonding** activities. It's encouraging that your teammates care and see your hard work!"
—**McKENNA**

"We have an annual '**pink-out,**' where our squad helps support a cure for breast cancer."
—**JULIA**

"Every homecoming, we **invite past cheerleaders to join us on the field** to cheer with us."
—**AIDAH**

"We do a **special ceremony** at cheer camp each year. We each bring one kind of bead, but enough for everyone. The bead is supposed to represent you. We light candles and go around in a circle, introducing ourselves and talking about why we cheer. After we talk, we pass our beads around the circle. In the end, everyone has a **cute beaded bracelet** and great memories."
—**BAILEY**

"Every year the upperclassmen and returners '**kidnap**' the underclassmen or newbies with parents' permission and take them to breakfast."
—**STARR**

"After school on Thursday, before the football game Friday, we **decorated the school** with streamers, signs, balloons, and posters! It was such an **amazing surprise** to everyone Friday morning!"
—**LINDSEY**

"During the practice closest to Halloween, we all **wear costumes** and try to cheer in our costumes. It's awesome seeing Captain America going up into a full, or a bumblebee throw a standing tuck."
—FORREST

"At every competition, my cheer team eats a Starburst and puts the wrapper in our right shoe for **good luck**. At the end of the competition, your sock is the color of your Starburst! We always remember that was the sock we wore to the competition."
—HEATHER

"On senior night at our high school, all the senior cheerleaders get to **cheer with tiaras** our coach gets them."
—JILLIAN

"At homecoming, guys dress up like girls and the **girls dress up like guys**."
—AUDREY

"We always would **hug the team teddy bear**, and after we performed we would sit in a circle and **hold hands** as a team."
—BETHANY

"My teammates and I huddle up before every game, performance, or tough practice and we also **dedicate our performance** to a specific individual, like a fan or former teammate. We also yell '*Vámonos Rayos*' ('Let's Go, Lightning') and '**Boom**' at the top of our lungs. It's probably my favorite part of the day."
—BETANIA

"Our **parents wear the team color** to our competitions and give us flowers."
—LEXII

about varsity

Since its founding in 1974 by Jeff Webb, Varsity has been the driving force in making cheerleading the dynamic, athletic, high-profile activity it is today. By combining high-energy entertainment with traditional school leadership, Webb and his organization have driven the development of an international phenomenon that now includes not only millions of young Americans but also a rapidly growing number of participants worldwide.

In 1979, Webb launched Varsity Spirit Fashion. It has become the world's largest designer and manufacturer of cheerleading and dance team apparel, combining the Varsity tradition of excellence with design innovation to help athletes perform at their best.

Today, Varsity is made up of the leading organizations and brands in all facets of cheerleading, including educational camps and clinics, competitions, and uniforms. Every year, Varsity trains more than 300,000 cheerleaders on fundamentals, with a major emphasis on safety. Camps and competitions are held in every state. Varsity also hosts a variety of national championships, from junior high to college level, five of them near the Walt Disney World® Resort near Orlando, Florida. ESPN has televised these national competitions for more than twenty-five years.

Varsity created the America Needs Cheerleaders campaign to encourage cheerleaders to be leaders on and off the field, especially by becoming involved in their communities. As stewards of cheerleading, Varsity celebrates cheerleaders and wants to spread the word about the magic cheerleaders create in the lives of others. The America Needs Cheerleaders campaign promotes all the values encouraged through cheer, such as leadership, spirit, commitment, kindness, and motivation.

Varsity has built a strong legacy of philanthropy, supporting organizations such as St. Jude Children's Research Hospital, the MDA telethon, the Make-A-Wish Foundation, and many others.

While Varsity's heritage is rich and its traditions renowned, it continues to be the innovative global leader in growing cheerleading's influence and profile. The organization's commitment to the health and well-being of the young people who participate is embedded in Varsity's high-quality educational curriculum and leadership in establishing instructional safety standards.

WHAT CAN VARSITY DO FOR YOU?

Varsity can help you and your squad with almost every aspect of cheerleading. Visit **varsity.com** to learn about options for camps and competitions, choose uniforms, explore community service opportunities and fundraising options, and watch amazing cheerleading videos on Varsity TV. You'll be inspired! The site also includes plenty of in-depth information on the topics covered in this book, and more. Subscribe to *American Cheerleader* magazine to become the best cheerleader you can be, with sideline tips, step-by-step skill instruction, and inside info on your favorite teams, along with cheerleading advice and the latest news and fashion from *real* cheerleaders just like you.

HOW CAN YOU GET INVOLVED WITH VARSITY?

Stay connected to Varsity through social media for the absolute latest on all things cheer! Through varsity.com, you can also nominate cheerleaders and squads for awards, ask questions of cheer experts, take online polls, and even explore career opportunities at Varsity.

acknowledgments

THANK YOU!

A big thank-you to all the **cheerleaders**, **coaches**, and **judges** whose voices and photos appear in these pages.

And thank you to the **Varsity Spirit team** who contributed their cheer knowledge and time to the project.

Thank you to photographers **Walt Beasley**, **Travis Cobb**, **Colin Dunn**, **Ryan Hicks**, **Jeff Jacoby**, **Steve Jones**, **Bill Sallaz**, **Chris Schubert**, and **Cassie Wright**.

Rebecca Webber gives special thanks to **Mary Nguyen Silsbee**, whose smile always lit up the stadium.

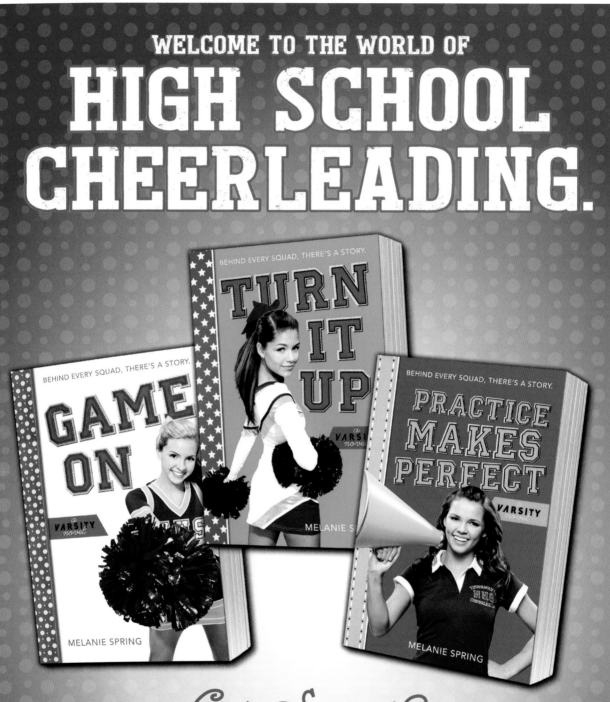